# The Law Commission
Consultation Paper No 196

# PUBLIC SERVICES OMBUDSMEN

# A Consultation Paper

ISBN: 9780118404945

Printed in the UK for The Stationery Office Limited
on behalf of the Controller of Her Majesty's Stationery Office

ID 2386040          09/10

Printed on paper containing 75% recycled fibre content minimum.

# THE LAW COMMISSION – HOW WE CONSULT

**About the Law Commission**

The Law Commission was set up by section 1 of the Law Commissions Act 1965 for the purpose of promoting the reform of the law.

The Law Commissioners are: The Rt Hon Lord Justice Munby (*Chairman*), Professor Elizabeth Cooke, Mr David Hertzell, Professor David Ormerod[1] and Miss Frances Patterson QC. The Chief Executive is: Mr Mark Ormerod CB.

**Topic of this consultation**

This consultation paper deals with the public services ombudsmen.

**Impact assessment**

An impact assessment is included in Appendix A.

**Scope of this consultation**

The purpose of this consultation is to generate responses to our provisional proposals.

**Duration of the consultation**

We invite responses from 2 September 2010 to 3 December 2010.

---

**How to respond**

**By email to:**     ombudsmen@lawcommission.gsi.gov.uk

**By post to:**     Public Law Team, Law Commission, Steel House, 11 Tothill Street, London, SW1H 9LJ

　　　　　　　Tel: 020-3334-0262 / Fax:    020-3334-0201

If you send your comments by post, it would be helpful if, wherever possible, you could send them to us electronically as well (for example, on CD or by email to the above address, in any commonly used format.

---

**After the consultation**

In the light of the responses we receive, we will decide our final recommendations and we will present them to Parliament. It will be for Parliament to decide whether to approve any changes to the law.

**Code of Practice**

We are a signatory to the Government's Code of Practice on Consultation and carry out our consultations in accordance with the Code criteria (set out on the next page).

**Freedom of information**

We will treat all responses as public documents in accordance with the Freedom of Information Act and we may attribute comments and include a list of all respondents' names in any final report we publish. If you wish to submit a confidential response, you should contact us before sending the response. PLEASE NOTE – We will disregard automatic confidentiality statements generated by an IT system.

**Availability of this consultation paper**

You can view/download it free of charge on our website at: **http://www.lawcom.gov.uk/docs/cp196.pdf**.

---

[1]    Professor Jeremy Horder was a Law Commissioner at the time this paper was drafted and approved. He was succeeded by Professor David Ormerod on 1 September 2010

# CODE OF PRACTICE ON CONSULTATION

o **THE SEVEN CONSULTATION CRITERIA**

**Criterion 1:    When to consult**

Formal consultation should take place at a stage when there is scope to influence the policy outcome.

**Criterion 2:    Duration of consultation exercise**

Consultations should normally last for at least 12 weeks with consideration given to longer timescales where feasible and sensible

**Criterion 3:    Clarity and scope of impact**

Consultation documents should be clear about the consultation process, what is being proposed, the scope to influence and the expected costs and benefits of the proposals.

**Criterion 4:    Accessibility of consultation exercises**

Consultation exercises should be designed to be accessible to, and clearly targeted at, those people the exercise is intended to reach.

**Criterion 5:    The burden of consultation**

Keeping the burden of consultation to a minimum is essential if consultations are to be effective and if consultees' buy-in to the process is to be obtained.

**Criterion 6:    Responsiveness of consultation exercises**

Consultation responses should be analysed carefully and clear feedback should be provided to participants following the consultation.

**Criterion 7:    Capacity to consult**

Officials running consultations should seek guidance in how to run an effective consultation exercise and share what they have learned from the experience.

o **CONSULTATION CO-ORDINATOR**

The Law Commission's Consultation Co-ordinator is Phil Hodgson.

o   You are invited to send comments to the Consultation Co-ordinator about the extent to which the criteria have been observed and any ways of improving the consultation process.

o   **Contact:**    Phil Hodgson, Consultation Co-ordinator, Law Commission, Steel House, 11 Tothill Street, London SW1H 9LJ – Email: phil.hodgson@lawcommission.gsi.gov.uk

**Full details of the Government's Code of Practice on Consultation are available on the BIS website at http://www.bis.gov.uk/policies/better-regulation/consultation-guidance.**

# THE LAW COMMISSION

# PUBLIC SERVICES OMBUDSMEN

## CONTENTS

100624926?

# PART 1
# INTRODUCTION

1.1 This Part sets out the origins of this consultation paper, delineates what we see as its proper scope and explains the structure we have adopted for it.

## ORIGINS OF THIS CONSULTATION PAPER

1.2 The starting point for this consultation paper was our project on administrative redress. The Ninth Programme on Law Reform in 2005 made provision for a scoping paper on the subject of remedies in judicial review and administrative law. We published that scoping report in 2006 and suggested that we address the following general question:[1]

> When and how should the individual be able to obtain redress against a public body that has acted wrongfully?

1.3 We published our consultation paper in July 2008 entitled *Administrative Redress: Public Bodies and the Citizen.*[2] This was followed by a report in May 2010.[3] The consultation paper considered three primary aspects of administrative redress: judicial review, private law actions against public bodies, and ombudsmen. The first two aspects of the project, which together could be seen as court-based actions for state liability, were discontinued in our report of May 2010.[4] In relation to ombudsmen the original consultation paper made four provisional proposals:

(1) the creation of a specific power to stay an application for judicial review, so that suitable matters are handled by ombudsmen rather than the courts;

(2) that access to the ombudsmen could be improved by modifying the "statutory bar" – the rule that recourse may not be had to the ombudsmen if the complaint has or could be pursued in a court of law;

(3) a power for the ombudsmen to refer a question on a point of law to the courts; and

(4) the removal of the MP filter in relation to the Parliamentary Commissioner for Administration, to allow a complainant direct access to the ombudsman without having to submit the complaint to a Member of Parliament.

1.4 Our provisional proposals met with generally favourable consultation responses. However, certain consultees thought that our initial proposals needed to be developed further. During consultation other issues came to light that we felt were

---

[1] Remedies against public bodies: A scoping report (10 October 2006) para 5.1.

[2] Administrative Redress: Public Bodies and the Citizen (2008) Law Commission Consultation Paper No 187 (hereafter CP 187).

[3] Administrative Redress: Public Bodies and the Citizen (2010) Law Commission No 322.

[4] Above, for the reasoning behind this discontinuance.

worth investigation. In our report of May 2010, we stated our intention undertake further work on the public services ombudsmen and publish the present consultation paper.

## SCOPE OF THIS CONSULTATION PAPER

1.5    The general scope of this consultation paper concerns what we have termed the public services ombudsmen. We consider them individually and set out their basic features in Part 2. Before that, however, we think it is worth considering what we mean by an ombudsman. The term ombudsman has come to be applied to a large number of bodies. These range from those bodies that an observer would naturally consider to be ombudsmen, to others where the application of the term may be less appropriate.

1.6    We do not think it is appropriate here to launch into an academic discussion of the various different definitions that have been suggested for an ombudsman, nor are we going to suggest one ourselves. However, we do suggest that there are certain key features to ombudsmen which taken together help differentiate them from other mechanisms for dispute resolution

1.7    First, whether as a result of a complaint or of its own motion, the ombudsman process is *investigatory*. This, to us, is probably the key to understanding ombudsmen. There is much that follows from this. Ombudsmen need sufficient powers to make the investigatory process effective. As we discuss in more detail later in this consultation paper, their investigatory process allows for different practices relating to disclosure to be put in place than those available to the courts.

1.8    Second, ombudsmen should be *independent*. Ombudsmen need to be seen as independent arbiters of the complaints put to them. They should not be seen as beholden to the bodies over which they have jurisdiction. Cabinet office guidance accepts this and states that a scheme should not be labelled an ombudsman scheme if not separated from the body it is reviewing.[5] This guidance mirrors that of the British and Irish Ombudsman Association.[6]

1.9    Third, ombudsmen make *recommendations*. The ombudsman approach is of a different nature to that of courts or tribunals. An ombudsman's report, or similar publication, does not have the force of law and does not coerce, at least in a strict legal sense, the body complained of into a particular course of action. This is not to say that the ombudsman approach is ineffective. As we will see later in this consultation paper, the implementation level of recommendations made by the public services ombudsmen is high. However, this is not the result of legal coercion but the political or moral pressure that a report places on a body to rectify injustice.

---

[5]    Cabinet Office, *Ombudsman schemes – guidance for departments* (2009).

[6]    The British and Irish Ombudsman Association offers the following four criteria to assess whether a body is an ombudsman: independence of the ombudsman from those whom the ombudsman has the power to investigate; effectiveness; fairness; and public accountability. See http://www.bioa.org.uk/criteria.php (last visited 16 August 2010).

1.10    Fourth, and this is specific to ombudsmen investigating the activities of public bodies, the primary focus of an ombudsman's jurisdiction and subsequent investigation is different to that of other redress bodies, such as courts or tribunals. An ombudsmen's primary focus is on *administrative processes*, the maladministration of which may have led to an individual suffering injustice. We accept that other mechanisms, particularly judicial review, also look at this issue. However, it is not the primary focus of judicial review – which is to assess the legality of a decision.

**The public services ombudsmen**

1.11    In this paper we have focused on what we term the public services ombudsmen. Given the range of ombudsmen now in existence in England and Wales, it was important for us to limit the scope of our research carefully. When we came to consider which ombudsmen it would be pertinent to investigate, we felt it appropriate to return to the original scope of the administrative redress project. That project, of which this is the last remaining part, focused on remedies against public bodies.

1.12    Our starting point was the general public services ombudsmen, which we take to mean the Parliamentary Commissioner for Administration, the Local Government Ombudsman and the Public Services Ombudsman for Wales. We note that the Collcutt review into the public sector ombudsmen in England considered only three ombudsmen: the Parliamentary Commissioner for Administration; the Commissioners for Local Administration; and, the Health Service Commissioners.[7] However, Collcutt was limited to England and our jurisdiction is England and Wales. Therefore it is necessary to include the Public Services Ombudsman for Wales.

1.13    If the Public Services Ombudsman for Wales is included then, given its role concerning social housing, the Independent Housing Ombudsman Scheme in England should also be included. In relation to social housing, we consider that the Independent Housing Ombudsman Scheme fulfils the role of a public services ombudsman.

1.14    Therefore, to us the appropriate bodies to fall within the category of public services ombudsmen are:

(1)    the Parliamentary Commissioner for Administration (the Parliamentary Commissioner);

(2)    the Commissioners for Local Administration (the Local Government Ombudsman);

(3)    the Health Service Commissioners (the Health Service Ombudsman);

(4)    the Public Services Ombudsman for Wales; and

(5)    the Independent Housing Ombudsman Scheme (the Housing Ombudsman).

---

[7]    Cabinet Office, *Review of the public sector ombudsmen in England* (2000).

1.15 We accept that our decision to include the Housing Ombudsmen is contentious given the mixed public/private nature of its jurisdiction. On balance we came to the view that it should be included.

**The fundamental institutional design of public services ombudsmen**

1.16 We decided against considering fundamentally changing the institutional design or identity of the public services ombudsmen. This consultation paper instead focuses on establishing what is at the core of the public services ombudsmen in our jurisdiction and what beneficial reforms could be made within that existing framework.

1.17 We accept that there is an imbalance in the models currently in place within the United Kingdom. The modern approach is for general public services ombudsmen, which is the model adopted in Wales and in Scotland. The Public Services Ombudsman for Wales handles matters that in England fall within the jurisdiction of the Local Government Ombudsman, the Health Service Ombudsman, the Housing Ombudsman and the Parliamentary Commissioner.

1.18 The Public Services Ombudsman for Wales and the Scottish Public Services Ombudsman are features of the devolution settlements. To create an ombudsman specific to the settlement was a logical course of action to take as part of the devolution process.

1.19 To advocate consolidating the existing Local Government Ombudsman, the Health Service Ombudsman and the social housing functions of the Housing Ombudsman would be outside the scope of the present project. Such an investigation would inevitably involve questioning the desirability of creating similar institutions for England as exist in Scotland and Wales. The original project was based on improving the work of existing institutions, not provisionally proposing the creation of new or different bodies.

1.20 Consequently, we do not think it appropriate in the context of this project to explore the matter further.

**Territorial considerations**

1.21 This sub-section considers territorial issues regarding the Law Commission and the Parliamentary Commissioner. These were raised in consultation on *Administrative Redress: Public Bodies and the Citizen*.

1.22 There is no United Kingdom legal jurisdiction. The United Kingdom comprises the three jurisdictions of England and Wales, Scotland, and Northern Ireland.

1.23 Acts of Parliament that apply throughout the United Kingdom in fact apply separately in the legal jurisdictions of England and Wales, Scotland, and Northern Ireland. This is the case with the Parliamentary Commissioner Act 1967, which extends to all three jurisdictions.[8]

---

[8] As it is silent as to extension to Scotland, it should be presumed to extend to Scotland: *Craies on Legislation* (8th ed 2009) para 11.1.2. It is specifically extended to Northern Ireland in Parliamentary Commissioner Act 1967, s13.

1.24 The Law Commission's ability to make recommendations is governed by the Law Commissions Act 1965, which limits our remit to "promoting the reform of the law of England and Wales".[9]

1.25 Our conclusion is that we can only propose changes to the law of England and Wales. In relation to Scotland and Northern Ireland, such provisional proposals as we make here form a commentary, to be taken up if so desired by those who have responsibility for those jurisdictions.

**Relationship with public bodies**

1.26 Increasingly intricate relationships are developing between the public services ombudsmen and elected bodies, specifically Parliament and the National Assembly for Wales.

1.27 There seem to us to be two aspects to the various relationships between the public services ombudsmen and elected bodies. First, oversight functions can be exercised by elected bodies. This can include a role in the appointment of the public services ombudsmen or in auditing their activity. Second, Parliament and the National Assembly for Wales are fora for the sort of political pressure that is necessary for implementation of ombudsmen recommendations.

1.28 This is an area where we, as the Law Commission, need to draw clear lines as to our responsibility. It is our role to propose reform of the *law*. This includes, for instance, the reform of the statutory provisions allowing public services ombudsmen to lay reports before Parliament or proposing a statutory role for Parliament or the National Assembly for Wales in the appointment of ombudsmen.

1.29 How Parliament and the National Assembly would choose to exercise such a statutory function is, constitutionally, a matter for them. We do not think it is our place to propose to Parliament, for instance, how it should order its select committees or how it should consider reports from the ombudsmen. Of course, a discussion of how Parliament might deal with such matters may be relevant considerations in assessing the desirability of statutory reform.

**THIS CONSULTATION PAPER**

1.30 This consultation paper is divided into eight Parts, including this introduction.

1.31 Part 2 sets out what we see as the core features of the public services ombudsmen.

1.32 Part 3 considers the regime for appointing the public services ombudsmen. This includes recent developments such as pre-appointment hearings before select committees of the House of Commons.

1.33 Part 4 focuses on issues relating to the opening of an investigation by the public services ombudsmen. This includes further consideration of the creation of a stay provision in the Administrative Court for ombudsmen, the modification of the statutory bar and the removal of the requirement that a complaint to the

---

[9] Law Commissions Act 1965, s 1(1).

Parliamentary Commissioner be forwarded by a Member of Parliament. These were included in our original consultation paper *Administrative Redress: Public Bodies and the Citizen.*

1.34   Part 5 looks at the procedures available to the public services ombudsmen when conducting an investigation into an individual complaint. This Part gives further consideration to the creation of a power whereby the public services ombudsmen can refer a question on a point of law to a court. This was originally included as a provisional proposal in our consultation paper *Administrative Redress: Public Bodies and the Citizen.*

1.35   In Part 6 we turn our attention to the results of investigations and the publication of individual and general reports by the public services ombudsmen. We consider the legal effect of the findings and recommendations of the public services ombudsmen in relation to the public body to whom they are addressed.

1.36   The final substantive Part, Part 7, returns to the relationship that the public services ombudsmen have with elected bodies such as Parliament and the National Assembly for Wales.

1.37   Part 8 collates the consultation questions asked in proceeding Parts.

1.38   Appendix A contains an impact assessment for this consultation paper.

# PART 2
# THE PUBLIC SERVICES OMBUDSMEN

## INTRODUCTION

2.1 In this Part we introduce the public services ombudsmen that we are considering in this project. We outline our thinking on ombudsmen in general and set out what we see as the primary functions of the public services ombudsmen. This forms the background to the substantive reforms which we provisionally propose in subsequent Parts.

## THE PUBLIC SERVICES OMBUSDSMEN

### Parliamentary Commissioner for Administration

2.2 The Parliamentary Commissioner was the first ombudsman to be established in the United Kingdom, following an influential report from JUSTICE in 1964.[1]

2.3 Setting out the general scheme for the Parliamentary Commissioner, the Government's initial White Paper on ombudsmen stated that:

> The fact that we are proposing this scheme does not mean that we think that the administration of Government departments is open to serious criticism or that injustices are frequently suffered by individual citizens. Far from it. We are in no doubt that the tradition of integrity and impartiality in our public administration is being fully maintained. But our proposal should increase confidence in that administration – by enabling complaints about administrative action to be fully and impartially investigated, so that, if a grievance is justified, it may be remedied, or, if it is unjustified, this may be demonstrated. It should also result, as has proved to be the case in other countries, in the further improvement of administrative standards and efficiency.[2]

2.4 Originally the Parliamentary Commissioner was portrayed as an adjunct to the constituency role of Members of Parliament. Introducing the second reading of the Parliamentary Commissioner Bill 1966, the Leader of the House put the function of investigations thus:

> The investigations of our Parliamentary Commissioner will in no way replace question time or the adjournment debate. On the contrary, they will provide the back bench Member ... with a new and powerful weapon which, up till now, neither he individually nor we collectively as a House has ever possessed— the possibility of impartial investigation into alleged maladministration.[3]

---

[1] JUSTICE, *The Citizen and the Administration: the redress of grievances* (1961) (the Whyatt report).

[2] White Paper, The Parliamentary Commissioner for Administration (1965) Cmnd 2767, para 15.

[3] *Hansard* (HC), 18 October 1966, vol 734, col 43.

The ombudsman focuses on central government departments and associated public bodies as are listed in schedule 2 of the Parliamentary Commissioner Act 1967.

2.5 Since coming into existence, and especially during its early years, the Commissioner has sometimes been portrayed as having failed to fulfil the vision that those in Justice had for it. Professor Bradley, writing in 1992, stated:

> The Parliamentary Commissioner is still suffering from the undue caution of the 1967 scheme and the remarkably effective way in which the Sir Humphreys of the 1960s insulated the Ombudsman from the public that he or she should serve.[4]

2.6 Some have complained that the Parliamentary Commissioner fails to attract sufficient cases.[5] Initially, the Commissioner did receive a smaller number of complaints than originally envisaged. However, in its most recent annual report, for 2008-09, the number of complaints received – 7,790 – exceeded those expected at its creation – 6,000 to 7,000.[6]

2.7 The post of the Parliamentary Commissioner is linked to that of Health Service Ombudsman and the incumbent is also the Health Service Ombudsman. However they are administered under different statutes.

**Local Government Ombudsman**

2.8 The institution of the Local Government Ombudsman was created by the Local Government Act 1974. Geoffrey Rippon MP, introducing the Local Government Bill 1973, explained their function thus:

> What we are doing, essentially, is to provide for local government a system for the investigation of maladministration akin to that established for central government in the Parliamentary Commissioner Act 1967, but tailored to the specific needs of local government. It does not represent a new worry or concern about the standards of administration or conduct in local government ... Provision of the system represents a general appreciation of the need to strengthen local democracy by giving a means whereby local issues of concern can be looked at quickly and dispassionately, and the opportunity for things that have gone wrong to be put right.[7]

2.9 The remit of the Local Government Ombudsman has continued to expand. The Health Act 2009, though not yet in force, will give the Local Government

---

[4] AW Bradley, "Sachsenhausen, Barlow Clowes – and then?" [1992] *Public Law* 353, 354.

[5] JUSTICE, *Our fettered ombudsman* (1977). See also, C Harlow and R Rawlings, *Law and Administration* (3rd ed 2009) ch 12.

[6] F Stacey, *Ombudsmen compared* (1978) p 129.

[7] *Hansard* (HC), 12 November 1973, vol 864 col 51.

Ombudsman the power to investigate complaints relating to privately arranged or funded adult social care.[8]

2.10   The Apprenticeship, Skills, Children and Learning Act 2009 gives the Local Government Ombudsman a role in complaints against the acts of governing bodies of schools and the exercise of, or failure to exercise, a "prescribed function" by the head teacher of a school.[9] There are three trials taking place at present, with the intention being to extend the jurisdiction across England in September 2011.

### Public Services Ombudsman for Wales

2.11   The Public Services Ombudsman (Wales) Act 2005 established the Public Services Ombudsman for Wales, unifying four existing bodies: the Local Government Ombudsman for Wales, the Health Service Ombudsman for Wales, the Welsh Administration Ombudsman and the Social Housing Ombudsman for Wales.

2.12   This is the most modern of the public services ombudsmen statutes in existence in the United Kingdom. It represents the last word the Government has had on the most appropriate structure for ombudsmen.

2.13   The Public Services Ombudsman for Wales has a broader jurisdiction than the proceeding two ombudsmen. Modelled on the Scottish Public Services Ombudsman,[10] it also investigates complaints relating to health and social housing provision in Wales.

2.14   We now turn to two sector-specific ombudsmen.

### Health Service Ombudsman

2.15   The primary task of the Health Service Ombudsman is to consider complaints relating to potential maladministration within heath care provision.

2.16   The Health Service Ombudsman's jurisdiction is limited to England. The NHS bodies subject to its jurisdiction are listed in section 2 of Health Service Commissioners Act 1993.

### Housing Ombudsman

2.17   Finally we turn to the Independent Housing Ombudsman Scheme, which was established under the Housing Act 1996. This is slightly different from the other public services ombudsmen we have considered, however we still think that it should be treated as a public services ombudsman.

2.18   The Housing Ombudsman is an officer of an independently established company, Independent Housing Ombudsman Limited, eligible to run an approved scheme under section 51 and schedule 2 of the Housing Act 1996. The scheme shares

---

[8]   Health Act 2009, s 35 and sch 5. It was originally intended that this would come into force in September 2010.

[9]   Apprenticeships, Skills, Children and Learning Act 2009, s 206.

[10]   Established by the Scottish Public Services Ombudsman Act 2002, s 1.

some features with a normal company; the articles of association create a board of directors. However, the Housing Act 1996 grants certain residual powers to the Secretary of State and any scheme must be approved by the Secretary of State before it can take on the role accorded it by the Act.

2.19    Social landlords must be members of the Housing Ombudsman scheme.[11] Social landlords are defined in section 51(2) of the Housing Act 1996 as:

(1)    a private registered provider of social housing,

(2)    a transferee of housing pursuant to a qualifying disposal under section 135 of the Leasehold Reform, Housing and Urban Development Act 1993;

(3)    a body which has acquired dwellings under Part 4 of the Housing Act 1988 (change of landlord: secure tenants); or

(4)    any other which was at any time registered with the Regulator of Social Housing or the Housing Corporation… and which owns or manages publicly-funded dwellings.[12]

The Housing Ombudsman's jurisdiction is limited to England.

## OVERVIEW OF THE OMBUDSMAN PROCESS: THREE COMMON FEATURES

2.20    In this section, we set out briefly certain features that are broadly similar across the public services ombudsmen. This is to help the reader with the subsequent Parts of the consultation paper, where we go into greater detail relating to the ombudsman process.

### Investigations

2.21    As we suggested above, at the core of the ombudsman process is the fact that it is investigatory. Investigations can also be undertaken by Royal Commissions or inquiries under the Inquiries Act 2005 or a wide range of other processes.

2.22    Cecil Clothier, writing in 1996,[13] sought to draw a distinction between the fact-finding inquiry process of an ombudsman and that of a large scale inquiry such as the Scott Inquiry into arms sales to Iraq.[14] Part of this relates to the mechanism adopted. The Scott Inquiry was focused on legal issues and involved lawyers, whereas the investigatory process adopted by the ombudsmen is intended to be much more informal. Part of Clothier's argument, however, relied on the scale of the enquiry and this assertion does not seem to have stood the test of time. In 1996, the ombudsman also published his report on the Barlow

---

[11]    Housing Act 1996, sch 2, para 1(1).

[12]    This definition was amended by the Housing and Regeneration Act 2008 (Consequential Provisions) Order 2010, SI 2010 No 866, sch 1, para.8.

[13]    C Clothier, "Fact-finding in inquiries – the PCA's perspective" [1996] *Public Law* 384. Cecil Clothier was the fourth Parliamentary Commissioner, from 1979 to 1984.

[14]    Report of the inquiry into the export of defence equipment and dual-use goods to Iraq and related prosecutions (1995-96) HC 115.

Clowes affair. If there ever was an argument as to the small-scale and non-political nature of ombudsmen's investigations then this is unsustainable after the recent *Occupational Pensions* and *Equitable Life* reports by the current Parliamentary Commissioner.[15] Both of these were very large-scale, costly investigations with wide ranging potential consequences.

2.23 However, what may be true for the Parliamentary Commissioner is not necessarily true for all of the public sector ombudsmen. Arguably, the other public services ombudsmen may have followed an approach closer to that suggested by Clothier for the Parliamentary Commissioner.

2.24 In part this could be the result of differences to the statutory frameworks of the public services ombudsmen. For instance, the Local Government Ombudsman cannot conduct an investigation into a matter "which in his opinion affects all or most of the inhabitants of the area"... "of the authority concerned".[16] There is no similar constraint on the most modern of the ombudsmen, the Public Services Ombudsman for Wales.

2.25 What it might be fairer to say is that large-scale investigations do not dominate the work of the public sector ombudsmen. Though there is the capacity for them to take on such a role, such work does not necessarily define them. We will return to this issue in greater depth in Part 5 of our consultation paper, where we consider whether this subject would benefit from reform.

2.26 An investigation by an ombudsman is administrative in nature. The complainant does not have a right of intervention, and there is no adversarial aspect to the process. The complainant and the relevant public bodies can, however, be invited to make submissions by the ombudsman. The process is meant to be informal.

2.27 Section 7(2) of the Parliamentary Commissioner Act 1967 requires that investigations should be conducted in private. Similar provisions exist in the governing statutes of the other public services ombudsmen.

2.28 Having a private process allows for a different approach to the release of documents and especially public interest immunity. The provisions in the Parliamentary Commissioner Act 1967[17] were far more generous in relation to the documents which would be released to the Parliamentary Commissioner than was the situation with respect to courts at the time.[18] However, certain classes of

---

[15] Trusting in the pensions promise: government bodies and the security of final salary occupational pensions, Report of the Parliamentary and Health Service Ombudsman (2005-06) HC 984 (*Occupational Pensions*); Equitable Life: a decade of regulatory failure, Report of the Parliamentary and Health Service Ombudsman (2007-08) HC 815.

[16] Local Government Act 1974, s 26(7).

[17] For instance that contained in the Parliamentary Commissioner Act 1967, s 8(3).

[18] In 1967, classes of documents could be withheld by the equivalent of a Public Interest I0.mmunity certificate: *Duncan v Cammell Laird* [1942] AC 624. This changed the following year in *Conway v Rimmer* [1968] AC 910. However, the position was still much less in favour of disclosure than was the case for the Parliamentary Commissioner.

documents, such as Cabinet papers, remained outside the approach to disclosure contained in the Parliamentary Commissioner Act 1967.[19]

2.29 As an interesting example of the difficult dividing line between evidence which should be released to the Parliamentary Commissioner and that which should not, we can consider the *Court Line* investigation. This investigation concerned the collapse of a group of companies including a holiday firm which was being monitored by the Government of the day. Some of the papers for the events that led up to the potential maladministration were Cabinet papers. It had always been the intention to restrict the Parliamentary Commissioner's access to such papers, as the Leader of the House had explained in the second reading of the Bill debate. However, in *Court Line* a compromise was reached, with the gist of the Cabinet papers being given to the Parliamentary Commissioner so that he could complete his enquiry and report on the issue.[20]

2.30 We are going to revisit the issue of the closed nature of the ombudsman process in Part 5 of this consultation paper, and put forward some provisional proposals for reform.

### Maladministration

2.31 Maladministration has been the subject of much academic discussion, and was deliberately left undefined in the statutes governing the public services ombudsmen.[21] Instead the ombudsmen were to define the term themselves through the course of their investigations.

2.32 The concept of maladministration first appeared, for the purposes of UK law, in the Franks Inquiry that followed on from the Critchell Down affair.[22] This concerned the mis-selling and resale of land by the Minister and officials in the Ministry of Agriculture.

2.33 The original Whyatt Report, which led to the establishment of the Parliamentary Commissioner, took the approach of considering what maladministration did not apply to. Therefore it was not to mean *bad* laws, or even the *wrong* policy.[23] In both of these cases the political process was the appropriate recourse, not an ombudsman. Whyatt also drew a distinction between a complaint of maladministration and one against a discretionary decision legally made within that discretion.[24]

2.34 The classic statement regarding maladministration however, was made by the Leader of the House in the second debate on the Parliamentary Commissioner

---

[19] For instance the proceedings of Cabinet or its committees: Parliamentary Commissioner Act 1967, s 8(4).

[20] Fifth Report of the Parliamentary Commissioner for Administration (1974-75) HC 498 (*Court Line*).

[21] See G Marshall, "Maladministration" [1973] *Public Law* 32; DW Williams, *Maladministration for injustice* (1976); KC Wheare, *Maladministration and its remedies* (1973).

[22] Report of the Committee on Administrative Tribunals and Enquiries (1957) Cmnd 218 (the Franks Committee).

[23] JUSTICE, *The Citizen and the Administration: the redress of grievances* (1961) para 70.

[24] Above, para 74.

Bill 1967. Richard Crossman MP set out his explanation to the House of Commons in two parts (thought frequently the first is ignored in favour of concentrating on the "catalogue" in the second):

> What about the definition of maladministration? In the first place I can define it to some extent negatively. It does not extend to policy, which remains a matter for Parliament. Nor do we include under maladministration that whole group of discretionary decisions which Sir John Whyatt treated separately in the first part of his report. Discretionary decision, properly exercised, which the complainant dislikes but cannot fault the manner in which it was taken, is excluded by this clause.
>
> A positive definition of maladministration is far more difficult to achieve. We might have made an attempt in this clause to define, by catalogue, all of the qualities which make up maladministration, which might count for maladministration by a civil servant. It would be a wonderful exercise – bias, neglect, inattention, delay, incompetence, inaptitude, perversity, turpitude, arbitrariness and so on. It would be a long and interesting list.[25]

2.35 In *R v Local Commissioner for Administration ex parte Bradford Metropolitan City Council*,[26] Lord Denning MR endorsed a passage from Wade's Administrative Law which contained the Crossman "catalogue" quoted directly from Hansard.[27]

2.36 In *R v Local Commissioner for Administration ex parte Eastleigh Borough Council*, Lord Donaldson MR noted that maladministration had been discussed in *ex parte Bradford*, and that all three judges in that case had come to differing views. Giving his own opinion, he went on to state that:

> In substance each was saying the same thing, namely, that administration and maladministration in the context of the work of a local authority is concerned with the *manner* in which decisions by the authority are reached and the *manner* in which they are or are not implemented. Administration and maladministration have nothing to do with the nature, quality or reasonableness of the decision itself.[28]

---

[25] *Hansard* (HC), 18 October 1966, vol 734, col 51.

[26] *R v Local Commissioner for Administration for the North and North East Area of England ex parte Bradford Metropolitan City Council* [1979] QB 287, 311H.

[27] HWR Wade, *Administrative Law* (4th ed 1977) p 82.

[28] *R v Local Commissioner for Administration ex parte Eastleigh Borough Council* [1988] QB 855, 863E.

2.37 Interestingly, the original Wyatt Report recognised the potential overlap between maladministration and the then existing remedies by way of judicial review – or a criminal action against a public body.[29] However as Lord Justice Henry put it in *Local Commissioner ex parte Liverpool City Council* when talking about the Local Government Ombudsman:

> What may not have been recognised back in 1974 was the emergence of judicial review to the point where most if not almost all matters which could form the basis for a complaint of maladministration are matters for which the elastic qualities of judicial review might provide a remedy.[30]

2.38 This is a topic to which we return in Part 4 as this overlap has grown, with potentially detrimental effects on access to ombudsmen.

2.39 As Crossman suggested in his statement to the House, section 12(3) (as it became) of the Parliamentary Commissioner Act 1967 limits the extent to which the Parliamentary Commissioner should interfere in the exercise of discretion or the merits of a decision made lawfully and without maladministration. Section 12(3) provides that:

> It is hereby declared that nothing in this Act authorises or requires the Commissioner to question the merits of a decision taken without maladministration by a Government department or other authority in the exercise of a discretion vested in that department or authority.

2.40 Sir Edmund Compton, the first Parliamentary Commissioner, used the presence of section 12(3) to bolster his argument that the statute did not envisage allowing "government by Commissioner".[31] Similarly to Whyatt and Crossman he discussed a bad discretionary decision which was not maladministration. His desire to keep within the limits of the statute could be seen in his reticence to become involved in such a matter, even where it caused hardship. He stated that it was the job of the department, not the Parliamentary Commissioner, to review such a rule.[32] This would seem to keep certain activity purely within the political sphere.

2.41 In examples considered later in this consultation paper, we can see that the boundaries of non-interference with discretion have been pushed. However, we are of the opinion that the starting premise is correct and that it is inappropriate to attempt to pin down maladministration.

---

[29] JUSTICE, *The Citizen and the Administration: the redress of grievances* (1961) para 73.

[30] *R v Local Commissioner for Administration in North and North East England ex parte Liverpool City Council* [2001] 1 All ER 462 at [23].

[31] Sir Edmund Compton was the first Parliamentary Commission for Administration, from 1967 to 1971. Prior to that he was Comptroller and Auditor General.

[32] E Compton, "The Parliamentary Commissioner for Administration" [1968] *Journal of the Society of Public Teachers of Law* 101, 111.

**Injustice**

2.42 Along with maladministration, a recurring concept in the governing statutes of public services ombudsmen is that of injustice. A finding of maladministration is not, of itself sufficient for a public services ombudsman to recommend a remedy.[33] There needs to be injustice resulting from the maladministration. However, as with maladministration, injustice was left undefined in the governing statutes. Both the public services ombudsmen and the courts have therefore come to interpret injustice broadly.[34]

2.43 For instance, in *R v Parliamentary Commissioner for Administration ex p Balchin (No 2)* the Administrative Court quashed the Parliamentary Commissioner's finding that the maladministration had not caused injustice. The Court concluded that the sense of outrage felt by the complainant had not been addressed.[35]

**CONCLUSIONS**

2.44 In closing this Part we draw some conclusions as to the primary functions of the public services ombudsmen. These help inform the discussion that takes place later in this consultation paper and the provisional proposals we make subsequent to that discussion.

2.45 In an early article on the ombudsman in 1968, Sir Edmund Compton highlighted three "credit items" to the work of the Parliamentary Commissioner. The first is having cases of maladministration detected and put right. In relation to this Compton confidently asserted that "the Parliamentary Commissioner and Whitehall are not adversaries: they are on the same side".[36] The second is having claims investigated by an independent authority allowed for the final disposal of unmeritorious claims. The third he suggested is that there is a tonic effect to the presence of a Parliamentary Commissioner upon the quality of Government administration. Here he drew a direct parallel with the work of parliamentary audit – he had formally been the Comptroller and Auditor General.

2.46 Almost twenty-five years ago, Cecil Clothier argued that there was value to ombudsmen in complex societies.[37] The core of his argument was that an ombudsman, and he also focused on the Parliamentary Commissioner for Administration, fulfils a vital role in relation to remedying administrative injustice suffered by individuals. As such the ombudsman fulfils a role potentially different to that occupied by judicial review. However, he went further than that and

---

[33] M Seneviratne, *Ombudsmen: Public services and administrative justice* (2002) p 50.

[34] The governing case law is: *R v Parliamentary Commissioner for Administration ex p Balchin (No 1)* [1997] COD 146; *R v Commissioner for Local Administration ex p S* [1999] COD 126; and, *R v Parliamentary Commissioner for Administration ex p Balchin (No 2)* (2000) 79 P&CR 157.

[35] *R v Parliamentary Commissioner for Administration ex p Balchin (No 2)* (2000) 79 P&CR 157.

[36] E Compton, "The Parliamentary Commissioner for Administration" [1968] *Journal of the Society of Public Teachers of Law* 101, 108.

[37] C Clothier, "The value of an ombudsman" [1986] *Public Law* 204.

suggested that an "ombudsman's mission has better and more far reaching consequences than the mere correction of other people's mistakes".[38]

2.47    We suggest that the public services ombudsmen sit in a privileged position that can allow them to have a broad overview of service delivery across the public sector. This is the result of the nature of their investigative process, especially the public services ombudsmen's access to the administrative process and the range of behaviour captured by the term "maladministration".

2.48    On this basis, we would suggest that there are three primary functions of the public services ombudsmen.

2.49    First, *to address individual complaints*. This was the reason for the establishment of the ombudsmen and will, rightly, always be at the core of their work. Public services ombudsmen can be viewed as standing at the summit of a complaints pyramid, meeting a demand for an independent review where internal mechanisms have not satisfied the complainant. This would include allowing a public body to bring to a close an unmeritorious claim by reference to an independent arbiter.

2.50    Secondly, the public services ombudsmen are in a privileged position to *address systemic failures* that occur across the administrative landscape. Repeat investigations into the behaviour of public bodies allow them to build up a good picture of that behaviour. The ombudsmen's recommendation and reporting functions allow them to address issues in a way not open to courts – who are reliant on individual cases.

2.51    Third, the public services ombudsmen are in a position to *disseminate knowledge across governance networks*. This, we suggest is slightly different to addressing systemic failure. This is more about allowing for knowledge transfer and the spread of good practice across different parts of the administrative landscape. This can be through reporting on performance, setting out codes of practice or the creation of principles to aid and inform administrative behaviour.

---

[38]    C Clothier, "The value of an ombudsman" [1986] *Public Law* 204, 206.

# PART 3
# APPOINTMENT OF OMBUDSMEN

## INTRODUCTION

3.1 This Part concerns the appointment of ombudsmen. In it we consider the statutory provisions and recent developments relating to the appointment of the public services ombudsmen – such as the establishment of pre-appointment hearings by select committees of the House of Commons. In discussing whether any changes should be provisionally proposed in relation to appointment, we also consider recent academic research on the topic before drawing our final conclusions.

## STATUTORY PROVISIONS FOR THE APPOINTMENT OF THE PUBLIC SERVICES OMBUDSMEN

3.2 The appointment process for the Public Services Ombudsman for Wales accords the greatest role to its associated elected body. Paragraph 1 of schedule 1 to the Public Services Ombudsman (Wales) Act 2005 provides that the ombudsman should be appointed by the Queen on the nomination of the National Assembly for Wales. This was an alteration to the earlier position, whereby the Queen appointed the ombudsman on the recommendation of the Secretary of State after consulting the Assembly.[1]

3.3 The appointment of the current ombudsman, in 2008, was made following selection by a recruitment panel chaired by the Chair of the Assembly Finance Committee. The other panel members were Ann Abraham, the Parliamentary Commissioner and the Health Service Ombudsman for England; Dianne Bevan, Chief Operating Officer to the National Assembly for Wales; and Vivienne Sugar, acting as the Independent Assessor. The appointment was approved in committee.[2]

3.4 The Parliamentary Commissioner is appointed by the Queen on the advice of the Prime Minister. However, practice has developed that the candidate put forward by the Prime Minister should have the approval of the Leader of the Opposition, and the Chairman of the Public Administration Select Committee will also have been consulted.[3] The Health Service Ombudsman is also appointed by Her Majesty.[4]

---

[1] Public Services Ombudsman (Wales) Act 2005, sch 1, para 1 as originally enacted. Amended by the Government of Wales Act 2006, sch 10, para 86(2).

[2] The nomination was approved by the National Assembly for Wales in plenary session on the 23 January 2008: http://www.assemblywales.org/bus-home/bus-chamber/bus-chamber-third-assembly-rop.htm?act=dis&id=72080&ds=1/2008#anc4 (last visited 16 August 2010).

[3] C Harlow and R Rawlings, *Law and Administration* (3rd ed 2009) p 530.

[4] Health Service Commissioners Act 1993, sch 1, para 1.

3.5 The Local Government Ombudsman is appointed by the Queen on the recommendation of the Secretary of State, after consultation.[5] The statute is silent as to who should be consulted.

3.6 Section 10 of the Housing Act 1996 states that the approved scheme shall provide for the terms of appointment of the Housing Ombudsman, and that this needs to be approved by the Secretary of State. If the scheme does not provide for appointment, then the Secretary of State can appoint the ombudsman subject to such terms as he or she sees fit.

3.7 Within the current Independent Housing Ombudsman Scheme, paragraph 57 provides that the Housing Ombudsman is appointed by the board of Independent Housing Ombudsman Limited, subject to the approval of the Secretary of State. The Board consists of nine members drawn from member landlords, tenants and independents.[6]

## PRE-APPOINTMENT HEARINGS

3.8 In the last few years Parliament and Government have collaborated to increase the parliamentary scrutiny given to certain public appointments. Here, we summarise the development of pre-appointment hearings by select committees from the genesis of the idea to the current approach.

3.9 The idea of pre-appointment hearings was raised by the Public Administration Select Committee in 2003. The Select Committee highlighted that "in practice Parliament plays hardly any role in making appointments or supervising public patronage".[7] The Committee therefore recommended a general system of pre-appointment hearings. This was to follow the practice of the Treasury Select Committee, which had been holding hearings with those nominated to the Monetary Policy Commissioner of the Bank of England since 1998.

3.10 The appointments to which this procedure was to apply were to be agreed between ministers and the relevant select committees. Select committees would then decide whether they wished to hold a hearing in each individual case. The Public Administration Select Committee argued that the use of "letters of reservation" – stating a select committee's disagreement with the appointment – rather than full confirmation hearings would provide a sensible balance between parliamentary oversight and the politicisation of appointments.

---

[5] Local Government Act 1974, s 23(4).

[6] http://www.housing-ombudsman.org.uk/whoweare.aspx?nm=8 (last visited 16 August 2010). At present there are equal numbers from each group.

[7] Government By Appointment: Opening Up the Patronage State, Report of the Public Administration Select Committee (2002-03) HC 165, p 30.

3.11    In its 2007 Green Paper, *The Governance of Britain*,[8] the Government followed a similar line to that suggested by the Public Administration Select Committee, stating that:

> There are a number of positions in which Parliament has a particularly strong interest because the officeholder exercises statutory or other powers in relation to protecting the public's rights and interests.[9]

3.12    The Government therefore suggested that select committees should conduct pre-appointment hearings with Government nominees for key positions. The Green Paper stated that the hearings would be non-binding but would inform the minister in their decision whether to proceed with the appointment.

3.13    It was envisaged that a list of the appointments to be subject to the hearings would be drawn up and agreed with the Liaison Committee. Both the Parliamentary Commissioner and the Local Government Ombudsman featured in the Government's initial – and all subsequent – lists of examples suitable for pre-appointment hearings.[10]

3.14    The Public Administration Select Committee published a further report on pre-appointment hearings in 2008.[11] The Select Committee recognised the importance of clear procedures with regard to the conduct of pre-appointment hearings and the way in which committees' opinions should be communicated. It invited the Liaison Committee to provide guidance on these areas.

3.15    In 2008 the Liaison Committee issued a report in response to the Green Paper and the Public Administration Select Committee's reports on the issue.[12] Pre-appointment hearings (in addition to those already conducted by the Treasury Select Committee) commenced in the 2007-08 session of Parliament. The Liaison Committee listed three that occurred in the session.[13]

3.16    On 12 October 2009, the Communities and Local Government Select Committee met to interview the Government's preferred candidate for the office of Local Government Ombudsman.[14] The Committee questioned the nominee – Jane Martin – on both her professional competence and her independence. The

---

[8]    HM Government, The Governance of Britain (2007) CM 7170, paras 72 to 81.

[9]    Above, para 75.

[10]    Above, para 77.

[11]    Parliament and public appointments: Pre-appointment hearings by select committees, Report of the Public Administration Select Committee (2007-08) HC 152.

[12]    Pre-appointment hearings by select committees, Report of the Liaison Committee (2007-08) HC 384.

[13]    The work of committees in 2007-08, Report of the Liaison Committee (2008-09) HC 291, para 63. These were: the Chair of the Care Quality Commission, Chair of the Office for Legal Complaints and Chair of the House of Lords Appointments Commission.

[14]    Appointment of the Local Government Ombudsman and Vice-chair of the Commission for Local Administration in England, Report of the Communities and Local Government Select Committee (2008-09) HC 1012.

committee published its report on 19 October 2009 and "encourage[d] the Secretary of State to make the appointment".[15]

3.17 There are currently two potential lists of appointments subject to pre-appointment hearings at Westminster: that issued by the Cabinet Office[16] and that by the Liaison Committee.[17] Both include all of the public services ombudsmen except the Housing Ombudsman and the Public Services Ombudsman for Wales. Given the existence of a process for the nomination of the Public Services Ombudsman for Wales, we can see how there does not need to be a duplicate process at Westminster. There are no reasons given for not including the Housing Ombudsman, though it should be noted that he is not appointed by a Minister, or on the recommendation of a Minister, but by the board of Independent Housing Ombudsman Ltd – subject to the approval of the Secretary of State.

**Academic work on pre-appointment hearings**

3.18 In the autumn of 2009, the Cabinet Office and the Liaison Committee commissioned a research project from the Constitution Unit at University College London. The resulting work, by Peter Waller and Mark Chalmers, was annexed to the Second Report of Session 2009-10 from the Liaison Committee.[18]

3.19 The research showed that parliamentarians thought that the current system could be strengthened, or at least amended from the current position. However, views on the appropriate variation differed between parliamentarians.[19] Some thought that there should be a power of veto, some that a wider range of candidates should be heard – rather than merely the Government's preferred candidate. Others thought that a simpler solution would be to conduct post-appointment hearings, so that a select committee can explain "how we saw the role and its priorities".[20]

3.20 Candidates broadly accepted the hearing as part of the democratic process.[21] Officials were measured in their overall responses. Most officials saw little value in the process, though some could see the advantages in improving the legitimacy of an appointment.[22]

---

[15] Appointment of the Local Government Ombudsman and Vice-chair of the Commission for Local Administration in England, Report of the Communities and Local Government Select Committee (2008-09) HC 1012, para 22.

[16] Cabinet Office, *Pre-appointment hearings by select committee: Guidance for departments* (2009) appendix A.

[17] Pre-appointment hearings by select committees, Report of the Liaison Committee (2007-08) HC 384.

[18] The Work of Committees in Session 2008-09, Report of the Liaison Committee (2009-10) HC 426. The work was also published separately by the Constitution Unit. References here are to the Liaison Committee Report. The text is identical.

[19] Above, annex 3, paras 3.7.1 to 3.7.10.

[20] Above, annex 3, para 3.7.8.

[21] Above, annex 3, paras 3.12.1 to 3.12.3.

[22] Above, annex 3, paras 3.21.1 to 3.21.11.

3.21　In concluding their research, the authors suggested that:

> A key argument for hearings was based on a broad view that significant public appointments should have an additional degree of transparency by engaging Parliament in the process of making those appointments. This was assumed to have a wider benefit in terms of democratic transparency, recognising that the post-holders for the various roles subject to scrutiny were exercising considerable powers in the public interest.[23]

3.22　In their opinion, this result had been achieved and the system as it now operates is more transparent than the former closed process.[24]

3.23　When considering options for future change, the authors sought to draw a distinction between four possible approaches.[25]

(1)　A greater role for Parliament in general. This could include a power of veto or selection by select committees.

(2)　The status quo. This could, however, include minor, incremental modifications.

(3)　A slight step back. This could include the replacement of pre-appointment hearings with post appointment hearings.

(4)　A hybrid approach. This would give Parliament a greater role in a small number of appointments.

3.24　In considering the first of these, the authors highlighted the practical problems there would be in effectively handing selection over to the select committees. This included the fact that many of the posts reported to Ministers and drew their budgets from departmental funds.[26] The second and the third options would follow systems either currently in place or formerly in place. In relation to the hybrid approach, they stated that:

> The logic of this is that there is a particular type of public appointment where the post holder is by definition required to be critical of Government (and on some occasions Parliament) in performing their role effectively – in effect to be on the side of the citizen against those who hold power over them … Several of the posts already covered by the requirement for pre-appointment hearings would fall within this category, for example the Parliamentary Commissioner for Administration. [These have the characteristic of being] appointments where independence of Government is "part of the DNA" of the role.[27]

---

[23]　The Work of Committees in Session 2008-09, Report of the Liaison Committee (2009-10) HC 426, annex 3, para 5.2.1.

[24]　Above, annex 3, para 5.2.2.

[25]　Above, annex 3, para 6.1.3.

[26]　Above, annex 3, para 6.2.5.

[27]　Above, annex 3, para 6.5.2.

3.25 The authors of the Constitution Unit report did not make recommendations as to the correct approach to take.[28] In its Second Report of Session 2009-10, which published the research as a House of Commons paper, the Liaison Committee thought that:

> Whilst a range of views on the best way forward is reflected within the Liaison Committee we believe that our discussions with the Minister indicate that there is scope for incremental development on a consensual basis.[29]

3.26 In its Coalition Agreement, the current Government committed itself to strengthening "the powers of select committees to scrutinise major public appointments".[30]

## CONCLUSIONS AND PROVISIONAL PROPOSALS

3.27 This is an area in which the Liaison Committee and the Public Administration Select Committee have been particularly active. We think that pre-appointment hearings are a useful adjunct to the role of Parliament in relation to the appointment of the public services ombudsmen.

3.28 It is not within our remit to make provisional proposals relating to the internal mechanisms by which elected bodies organise themselves. However, the statutory provisions governing who makes appointments and who makes recommendations as to appointments are part of the law. Therefore this is a subject that falls within our competence.

3.29 It seems to us to be particularly appropriate to make Parliament the pivotal institution in the appointment of the Parliamentary Commissioner. This is because the Parliamentary Commissioner has always held itself out to be an aid to the work of Parliament. The practical concerns raised in the UCL Constitution Unit report do not apply in the case of the Parliamentary Commissioner – or, necessarily, in the case of the other public services ombudsmen.[31]

3.30 We do not think that the case for a pivotal role for Parliament in the appointment of either the Health Service Ombudsman or the Local Government Ombudsman is so strong. The necessity of Parliament's relationship with the Parliamentary Commissioner has been shown throughout its history. In part this is a result of the subject matter of its investigations.

3.31 Given the importance of independence from the Government, we think there is an argument for the Government to be completely divorced from any role in relation to the Parliamentary Commissioner. Accordingly, we suggest that the process for the selection of the Parliamentary Commissioner should be reformed.

---

[28] The Work of Committees in Session 2008-09, Report of the Liaison Committee (2009-10) HC 426, annex 3, para 6.1.2.

[29] Above, para 69.

[30] HM Government, *The Coalition: our programme for Government* (2010) p 21.

[31] The Chair of the Office of Budget Responsibility, a body which similarly covers the core work of Parliament (the control of monetary supply), is to be appointed with a veto power being held by the House of Commons Treasury Select Committee.

3.32    Our preliminary view is that it would be possible to strengthen the role of Parliament in appointing the Parliamentary Commissioner. We provisionally consider that it would be desirable to create a system whereby the Parliamentary Commissioner is nominated by Parliament.

3.33    We think that it might be necessary to include a procedure for default appointment by the Secretary of State in the event that Parliament is unable to nominate someone within a specified statutory time period.

3.34    On this basis, **we provisionally propose that Parliament nominate to the Queen a candidate for the post of Parliamentary Commissioner for Administration.**

3.35    It would, of course, be for Parliament to adopt such rules and processes as it thinks fit to achieve the ends encapsulated in any legislative change to section 1 of the Parliamentary Commissioner Act 1967. The way in which the National Assembly for Wales nominated the Public Services Ombudsman for Wales could be seen as a potential model. It would also be possible to envisage a select committee of the House of Commons, or indeed a joint committee of both Houses, making the necessary nomination.

3.36    The Housing Ombudsman is not on the list of appointments which are subject to pre-appointment hearings by select committees. This is despite the fact that it performs a function of comparable public importance to many on that list. We accept that any change to the current arrangement would probably mean that the appointment is made not by the board of Independent Housing Ombudsman Limited but by the Secretary of State. This, we suggest, would be worthwhile in order to improve transparency and accountability in the workings of the public services ombudsmen. However, this is an area which is properly within the internal workings of Parliament. Therefore we do not think it within our remit to make provisional proposals.

3.37    Finally, the relationship which the Public Services Ombudsman for Wales enjoys with the National Assembly for Wales is one of the more legislatively developed among the public services ombudsmen. Where it seems to depart from reforms currently underway in Parliament is in relation to pre-appointment hearings. It would be outside the scope of this project to consider whether these should be adopted for nominations from the National Assembly for Wales for appointments to be made by the Queen. However, we would like to draw consultees' attention to this issue in order to raise the level of general discussion on what is an important area. As with pre-appointment hearings for the Housing Ombudsman at Westminster, we are not going to make provisional proposals.

# PART 4
# OPENING AN OMBUDSMAN INVESTIGATION

## INTRODUCTION

4.1 This Part considers issues around the ability of an ombudsman to open an investigation. The investigatory process itself is dealt with in the next Part.

4.2 We consider the issues in relation to opening an investigation as falling under two broad headings. First, the effect of the existence of other mechanisms for handling the complaint on the public services ombudsmen's decision to open an investigation. Second, the formal requirements, outlined in the governing statutes for the public services ombudsmen, that need to be met before an investigation can be opened.

4.3 We have taken a policy decision, in accordance with our thinking on the functions of the public services ombudsmen, not to consider self-generated investigations. The primary task for the public services ombudsmen, as we see it, is dealing with complaints. There is a secondary function, relating to systemic failure, which is still dependant on complaints received.

4.4 We note that section 26B of the Local Government Act 1974 allows the Local Government Ombudsman to investigate matters wider than an initial investigation if matters come to light in the course of an initial investigation which may affect, or have already affected, others. However, this is still dependant on the original complaint and subsequent investigation.

4.5 In our 2008 consultation paper, *Administrative Redress: Public Bodies and the Citizen*,[1] we put forward provisional proposals in relation to what we refer to as the statutory bar, dedicated stay of proceedings and the MP filter. We consider the responses in this part.

## RELATIONSHIP WITH OTHER INSTITUTIONS FOR ADMINISTRATIVE JUSTICE

4.6 The public services ombudsmen have to fit within the general landscape for administrative justice. This means that general strictures relating to administrative law, for instance that complaints relating to service delivery should ideally be dealt with internally in the first instance, should be adhered to.

4.7 It also means that institutions occupying this landscape should have regard to each other and seek to allocate complaints between themselves in the most efficient and effective manner. For the purposes of this paper, the other relevant institutions are the Administrative Court, tribunals and alternative dispute mechanisms, such as mediation.

4.8 The Administrative Justice and Tribunals Council, established under the Tribunals, Courts and Enforcement Act 2007, published recently a set of

---

[1] CP187.

*Principles for Administrative Justice.*[2] These built on the work of others in the field, particularly the *Principles of Good Administration* published by the Parliamentary Commissioner and Health Service Ombudsman.[3] Relevant to this issue, the Administrative Justice and Tribunals Council states that a system for administrative justice should:[4]

(1) make users central – and always keep their needs in mind;

(2) lead to just and timely outcomes – correct decisions within timescales which meet the needs of users;

(3) treat people fairly and respectfully – having regard to individual circumstances; and

(4) work proportionately and efficiently – in offering routes to redress, in procedural requirements and in delivering value for money.

4.9 We suggest that these form a useful backdrop when considering the landscape for administrative justice and the various options contained therein.

4.10 Turning to specific institutional procedures, the first two that we considered were provisionally proposed in our consultation paper *Administrative Redress: Public Bodies and the Citizen*. These were the statutory bar and a dedicated stay of proceedings in judicial review in favour of the ombudsmen. In addition we consider, and propose specific mechanisms for, the public services ombudsmen encouraging alternative dispute resolution.

**The statutory bars**

4.11 In all of the governing statutes for the ombudsmen there are provisions which have the aim of preventing an ombudsman opening a complaint, where the complainant has previously had recourse to another institution for administrative justice.

4.12 The relevant provision for the Parliamentary Commissioner is section 5(2)(b) of the Parliamentary Commissioner Act 1967. This provides:

> (2) Except as hereinafter provided, the Commissioner shall not conduct an investigation under this Act in respect of any of the following matters, that is to say –
>
> (a) any action in respect of which the person aggrieved has or had a right of appeal, reference or review to or before a tribunal constituted by or under any enactment or by virtue of Her Majesty's prerogative;
>
> (b) any action in respect of which the person aggrieved has or had a remedy by way of proceedings in any court of law:

---

[2] Administrative Justice and Tribunals Council, *Principles for administrative justice: The AJTC's approach – consultation draft* (2010).

[3] Parliamentary and Health Service Ombudsman, *Principles of good administration* (2009).

[4] Administrative Justice and Tribunals Council, *Principles for administrative justice: The AJTC's approach – consultation draft* (2010) principles 1, 2, 5 and 6.

> Provided that the Commissioner may conduct an investigation notwithstanding that the person aggrieved has or had such a right or remedy if satisfied that, in the particular circumstances, it is not reasonable to expect him to resort or have resorted to it.

4.13 Section 9 of the Public Services Ombudsmen (Wales) Act 2005 provides that the ombudsman may not investigate a matter if the person aggrieved has or had "a remedy by way of proceedings in a court of law" but this does not apply where the ombudsman "is satisfied that, in the particular circumstances, it is not reasonable to expect the person to resort, or have resorted, to the right or remedy".

4.14 For the Local Government Ombudsman, section 26(6) of Local Government Act 1974 is phrased in almost identical terms, including the discretion. This is the same in section 4(1) of the Health Service Commissioners Act 1993.

4.15 The Housing Act 1996 is silent on this point. However, the following sub-clauses are contained in the governing rules for the Independent Housing Ombudsman Scheme, whereby the Housing Ombudsman will not investigate complaints which:

(1) Concern matters where proceedings have been issued or they have already been taken to a court or tribunal, where a complainant will have or has had the opportunity to raise them in the proceedings and where, in the case of proceedings started by a member landlord, the Ombudsman is satisfied that the proceedings are not designed to prevent his investigation of the complaint.

(2) Are matters where the Ombudsman considers it quicker, fairer, more reasonable, and more effective to seek a remedy through the courts, other tribunal or procedure.[5]

4.16 The Housing Ombudsman provisions are neither statutory nor written in exactly the same terms as those for the other public services ombudsmen. However, we suggest that the effect of them – at least as far as the recipients of publicly delivered services are concerned – is similar to the statutory provisions for the other public services ombudsmen.

4.17 The existence of these provisions is an acknowledgment that there are overlapping jurisdictions. In broad terms overlaps can exist because of the definition of maladministration. The area of overlap has therefore been enlarged as the grounds for review in judicial review have expanded in recent years. Maladministration, as we set out in Part 2, was left deliberately undefined in the governing statutes of the public services ombudsmen, so that the ombudsmen would define it on the basis of their own case law.

---

[5] Independent Housing Ombudsman Scheme, clause 16(e) and (f), available at http://www.housing-ombudsman.org.uk/downloads/HOS_Scheme.pdf (last visited 16 August 2010).

4.18 Subsequently, maladministration has been taken to include – amongst many other things:

  (1) corruption;

  (2) bias and unfair discrimination; and

  (3) making the decision on the basis of faulty information which should have been properly ascertained and assembled.[6]

4.19 These would also be grounds for judicial review. Consequently, at a fundamental level, there is a significant potential for overlap between the administrative justice institutions.

4.20 The effect of these provisions is to give a preference for the courts in those circumstances. Where there is an overlap then section 5(2)(b) of the Parliamentary Commissioner Act 1967, and similar provisions in the statutes of the other public services ombudsmen apply. These require the ombudsmen to decline jurisdiction unless it is not reasonable to expect the complainant to have resorted to an alternative path– be that the Administrative Court, tribunal or other appeal body.

4.21 Recent case law suggests that the discretion to accept a complaint does not extend to cases where an action for judicial review has been commenced. In *Umo*, the Administrative Court stated that:

> In a case where legal proceedings have in fact been instituted, the wording of the proviso precludes there being discretion in the local ombudsman to proceed thereafter.[7]

4.22 This case law concerns the Local Government Ombudsman. Whether the same principle applies to the Parliamentary Commissioner is not clear but the provisions for the Parliamentary Commissioner are identical to those for the Local Government Ombudsman.

4.23 One potential corollary of this preference is to place pressure on complainants to move towards confrontational litigation at an early date. This preference in favour of judicial review is reinforced by the limitation period of judicial review. This requires that an action should be commenced as soon as practicable, and in any event within three months of the decision objected to. In contrast a claimant has twelve months in which to bring a complaint to the ombudsman.[8]

---

[6] See H Woolf, J Jowell and A Le Sueur, *De Smith's Judicial Review* (2007) para 1-071.

[7] *R (Umo) v Commissioner for Local Administration in England* [2003] EWHC 3202 (Admin) at [17].

[8] Public Services Ombudsman (Wales) Act 2005, s 5(1)(b); Parliamentary Commissioner Act 1967, s 6(3); Local Government Act 1974, ss 26B(1)(a) and (2); Health Service Commissioners Act 1993, s 9(4). There is discretion to disapply this requirement in each of the governing statutes. The relevant provisions of the Housing Ombudsman Scheme, paras 16(a)(ii) and (iii), are drawn in similar terms.

4.24 Given recent developments in administrative justice[9] and the acceptance of the importance of ombudsmen – as demonstrated by their creation for the devolved administrations of Wales, Scotland and Northern Ireland – we do not think that the default position in favour of judicial review is sustainable.

*Consultation responses*

4.25 In our consultation paper *Administrative Redress: Public Bodies and the Citizen* we suggested that the current statutory bar should be reformed such that:

> An ombudsman may conduct an investigation, notwithstanding that the person aggrieved has or had a legal remedy, if in all the circumstances it is in the interests of justice to investigate.[10]

4.26 We listed four factors to be taken into account when taking a decision to investigate:

(1) The availability of statutory procedures.

(2) The nature of the complaint.

(3) The characteristics of the parties.

(4) The claimant's objectives.[11]

4.27 We asked two questions relating to this issue which we deal with separately below.

WHEN SHOULD THE STATUTORY BAR BE MODIFIED?

4.28 The first question that we asked was:

> Do consultees agree that the statutory bar should be modified both in cases where legal proceedings have been commenced and where there is a potential remedy before the court?[12]

4.29 Thirty-one responses commented on the statutory bar proposal. Twenty-six consultees favoured modification as proposed; five objected to it.

4.30 One consultee, Veronica Howard, drew attention to the injustice that can be caused where complainants fall into the jurisdictional gap between the ombudsmen and the court system. She argued for greater flexibility in the system and that ombudsmen should be able to:

> Consider a complaint where there are clearly issues that could not be addressed by the Government body who had dealt with the complaint originally [in this case the Planning Inspectorate].

---

[9] For instance the Tribunals, Courts and Enforcement Act 2007.

[10] CP 187, para 5.71.

[11] CP 187, paras 5.8 to 5.24.

[12] CP 187, para 5.75.

4.31    However, several consultees highlighted the potential resource implications of the proposals. Some noted that Government would need to ensure sufficient resources were provided and suggested that a wide-ranging funding review for ombudsmen be conducted.

4.32    Government was concerned that our proposals would result in more complaints before the ombudsmen. It noted that the statutory bar is an "important mechanism for preventing duplication between the courts and the ombudsmen", and that without it costs for the system may increase. However, the Government also accepted that "there may be confusion about when the existing discretion to disapply the statutory bar should operate".

DISCRETION AS THE DEFAULT POSITION

4.33    The second question that we asked was:

> Do consultees agree that this should be done so that the default position is that ombudsmen have discretion to investigate regardless of the availability of a legal remedy?[13]

4.34    Twenty-three responses agreed with the default position as proposed. One consultee, the Government, expressed concern that the proposal may result in considerable delay, especially in immigration and tax assessment cases:

> The Law Commission proposes to change [the current test] to a general interests of justice test that applies irrespective of whether the person has or had a legal remedy. The effect of this would be to give the complainant an additional avenue for redress (in this case, cost free to the complainant, although not to the public purse) which does not currently exist, and which might be used to create delay.

4.35    Amongst some consultees who agreed with the proposal there was some concern at the unstructured and broad nature of the discretion to investigate outlined in our proposals. Several suggested that it would be necessary to formulate a clearly structured discretion in order to avoid delay and duplication.

4.36    However, both the Local Government Ombudsman and the Parliamentary and Health Service Ombudsman, in their responses to the consultation, felt that concerns about delay were misplaced. The Local Government Ombudsman stated that ombudsmen were already alert to the issues of delay and would use their discretion not to initiate investigations in order to minimise these problems.

4.37    The Parliamentary and Health Service Ombudsman agreed with the default position, and argued further that:

> The greater danger at present is that complainants will fall through the "remedy gap" rather than find themselves spoilt for remedial choice.

---

[13]   CP 187, para 5.75.

### Conclusions and provisional proposals

4.38 Consultation responses to our original proposals were generally favourable and suggested that the abolition of the statutory bar is a useful course to pursue further.

4.39 We think that Government concerns in relation to any change causing the extra delay in administrative processes – such as deportation – are over-stated. There are no powers in the governing statutes that would prevent the process continuing – where this felt to be necessary by the public body.

4.40 On reflection and after consultation, we suggest that the question of whether it is appropriate for an ombudsman to investigate a matter should be entrusted to the ombudsmen – though with the normal oversight of the Administrative Court.

4.41 In 1967, there was a single, young and untested institution. There is now a family of experienced public services ombudsmen. The statutory provisions, though, are those of 1967. We suggest that the current rules that dictate particular conclusions to the ombudsmen and contain a preference in favour of courts are inappropriate within the current landscape of administrative justice.

4.42 Having conducted initial consultation, we remain of the opinion that the statutory bars for the public services ombudsmen should be reformed. However, on reflection, we would like to strengthen and simplify our initial approach. Therefore, **we provisionally propose that the existing statutory bars be reformed. We provisionally propose that there is a general presumption in favour of a public services ombudsman being able to open a complaint.**

4.43 Our original proposal was based around a mechanism that the public services ombudsmen should have to consider whether it is "in the interests of justice" to open an investigation – with reference to the four factors we listed above. However, we now think that if the ombudsman has jurisdiction, then there is, on the face of it, a good argument for opening an investigation.

4.44 By reversing the current bar the public services ombudsmen must consider the fact that a complainant has had, or may have, recourse to another mechanism for administrative redress.

4.45 We think this would be a suitable change as it would remove a troublesome barrier to jurisdiction. However, it would not create a new set of factors or procedures for the ombudsmen to consider – rather it would leave them with a simplified jurisdictional question.

4.46 We suggest that our proposed reform to the statutory bar and the creation of a dedicated power to stay and transfer cases to the ombudsmen – as detailed in the next section – emphasise the role of the Administrative Court as a mechanism of last resort. Reform of the statutory bars in their current form would remove a preference in favour of the Administrative Court where the public services ombudsmen are an equally viable option.

4.47 We therefore ask the following consultation questions:

(1) **Do consultees agree that there should be a general presumption in favour of the ombudsman being able to investigate a complaint coupled with a broad discretion to decline to open an investigation?**

(2) **Do consultees agree that in deciding whether to exercise their discretion to decline to open an investigation ombudsmen should ask themselves whether the complainant has already had or should have had recourse to a court or tribunal?**

### Dedicated stay of proceedings for ombudsmen

4.48 In our consultation paper we proposed a second mechanism to help the overall landscape of administrative justice work in an effective and efficient manner. This would be by ensuring that cases were allocated appropriately between the different institutions that occupy that landscape. The mechanism would be a dedicated stay in favour of the ombudsmen, available to the Administrative Court.

4.49 Our initial thinking was based around the idea that an action may come before the Administrative Court, where at the permission stage it can be seen that there is some underlying illegality such as to justify permission for judicial review. However, the true nature of the claim, taken as a whole, is one properly described as maladministration. Here, giving the Administrative Court a dedicated power to stay the proceedings would allow the core of the matter to be dealt with in the most appropriate way. If, after the ombudsman had considered the matter, it was still felt necessary to deal with the underlying illegality then the stay could be set aside and the claim's illegality tested in court.

### *Consultation responses*

4.50 In relation to the stay provision we asked two separate consultation questions. These will be taken in turn.

A STAY PROVISION AS A USEFUL TOOL?

4.51 The first question we asked was:

> Do consultees think a stay provision would be a useful tool in ensuring disputes are dealt with in the appropriate forum?[14]

4.52 Thirty-five responses commented on the stay provision. Twenty-four consultees agreed with the proposals, eleven disagreed.

4.53 Of those consultees who agreed with the proposals, several felt that they would encourage a greater use of the ombudsman with positive consequences. Richard Kirkham noted that it would redress the current preference in favour of judicial review, since:

> The three month time limit for judicial review often renders the ombudsman route an all or nothing option for the potential claimant.

---

[14] CP 187, para 5.38.

4.54 Mr Justice Sullivan[15] stated that many cases could be better dealt with by ombudsmen than the courts. In particular he noted that many claims involving health, social care or education services provision would be better handled in this way because:

> In such cases, where the public body will continue to be responsible for providing a service, so that the parties will have to "live with each other" following resolution of the dispute, the corrosive effects of adversarial litigation are most unfortunate.

4.55 Several consultees supported our proposal but stipulated various conditions that they felt would be necessary for the stay process to operate successfully. The Local Government Ombudsman argued that it should be clear that claims would only be allowed to return to court once the ombudsman route had been exhausted, and then only on a point of law. However, the Government envisaged that no further appeal would be allowed at all, and cautioned that the possibility of delay and costs implications would need to be considered. We did consider this point but returned to the fact that the point of the mechanism was to give the courts a broad discretion to allow matters to go to the ombudsmen only where that was in the interests of justice.

4.56 The Civil Procedure Rules make specific provision for the court to stay proceedings for the purposes of alternative dispute resolution for one month, or for such a period as it considers appropriate.[16] This may be at the request of the parties or at the court's own initiative where it considers that such a stay would be appropriate.[17]

4.57 Furthermore, if the court considers that there is an alternative remedy which ought to be exhausted, this may be considered a good reason to refuse permission or, to refuse relief where the issue arises at the substantive hearing,[18] The court also has a general case management power to stay proceedings in appropriate circumstances.

4.58 We accept that the court does have broad case management powers but these do not include the ability to stay a case in the circumstances outlined in paragraph 4.49 above. We suggest that such a mechanism would be of most value at the permission stage. Our aim was not to circumvent the rules on damages in judicial review but to allow a claim to be dealt with by the most appropriate mechanism for administrative justice.

---

[15] Now Lord Justice Sullivan.

[16] The court can extend the stay until such date, or for such a specified period as it thinks appropriate. Civil Procedure Rules, r 26.4(3).

[17] Civil Procedure Rules, r 26.4(2).

[18] M Fordham, *Judicial Review Handbook* (4th ed 2004) para 36.3. See also K Olley, "Alternative Remedies and the Permission Stage" [2000] *Judicial Review* 240.

## PROBLEMS WITH A STAY PROVISION

4.59 The second question we asked was:

> What problems do consultees see with the operation of the stay as described?[19]

4.60 Several consultees did not see the ombudsman as an informal alternative to court. Browne Jacobson LLP claimed that ombudsmen were more frequently used by "more educated" complainants and that public bodies' reliance on legal representation would disadvantage the less articulate complainant. The Advice Services Alliance raised concerns that a claimant might lose their representation under the stay procedure, where the legal aid certificate does not extend to ombudsman work.

4.61 In its consultation response the Government expressed the opinion that the stay procedure should require the consent of all the parties. A number of other consultees adverted to the possibility that, where the stay procedure was not consensual, a complainant may not be willing to engage with the ombudsman's investigation. The Public Law Project agued that since an ombudsman's investigation is dependant on interviews and the co-operation of the parties:

> If one party has not even accepted that the ombudsman should investigate, this would seriously undermine the effectiveness and validity of the investigation and its conclusions.

4.62 The Local Government Ombudsman agreed that a compulsory stay procedure could result in parties being unwilling to co-operate with their investigations. However, they did not feel that, in their own case, this would present a significant problem:

> If an individual whose case had been referred to a Local Government Ombudsman (LGO) refused to cooperate with our investigation to the point where the investigation was no longer fruitful, the LGO would have to consider using general discretion to discontinue his or her involvement, and the matter would then return to court.

4.63 Similarly the Administrative Justice and Tribunals Council agreed that a stay provision would be useful, but added that ombudsmen should retain their discretion whether to accept a complaint. The co-operation of the complainant could then be "an influential but not determinative factor in the exercise of that discretion".

4.64 A few consultees discussed the impact that the power to stay may have on the ombudsmen's procedures and resources. Mr Justice Silber agreed that the stay provision would be useful, and had only one reservation: "whether the ombudsmen have the capacity and resources to take on the additional cases". The Local Government Ombudsman also cautioned that the courts should have access to "accurate and authoritative advice and information on the ombudsman's jurisdiction before deciding on a stay and referral".

---

[19] CP 187, para 5.38.

4.65    York Law School noted that our proposals regarding the stay procedure had not included the county court. This would cause disparity in homelessness cases they said, where some decisions were appealed through judicial review and others went to the county court.

### Conclusions and provisional proposals

4.66    We remain of the opinion that a stay mechanism would be a useful additional tool, allowing for the proper allocation of cases between the Administrative Court and the public services ombudsmen. Given further reflection and consultation responses, we see this mechanism as being relevant primarily at the permission stage.

4.67    Though there are arguments that this should merely be a stay provision, leaving the question as to whether to open an investigation for the ombudsmen solely, we think that the provision should be stronger than that. We suggest that the proper relationship would be for a matter to be transferred to the ombudsmen from a court.

4.68    The initial decision would be made at the permission stage. As any stay and referral would be of importance to the parties, we suggest that they should have the opportunity to comment on this procedure.

4.69    We, therefore, consider that it would be appropriate for the court to adopt a procedure whereby it invites further submissions from the parties to the initial court-based action – where it is minded to transfer the matter.

4.70    We suggest that this could be dealt with by a suitable amendment to the Civil Procedure Rules or with a Practice Direction.

4.71    Subsequent to this, the public services ombudsman would be obliged to open an investigation. The procedure they adopted in doing so would remain theirs. The purpose of the mechanism is to allow a matter to be investigated by an ombudsman where the court feels this to be the most appropriate process. An ombudsman's investigation has a very different purpose and focus to those of pleadings before the initial court.

4.72    We accept York Law School's criticism. We think it right that a more general provision should be available to all such courts as have matters before them that could be properly categorised as maladministration. A court would still only be able to transfer a matter which is within the potential jurisdiction of the relevant public services ombudsman, and the power should be confined to judicial review-like proceedings, such as the county court jurisdiction on homelessness appeals.

4.73    We were guided in coming to this conclusion by amendments to the Senior Courts Act 1981. The Tribunals, Courts and Enforcement Act 2007 inserted section 31A into the Senior Courts Act 1981.[20] This provides that where an application is made to the High Court for judicial review, or for permission to apply for judicial review, then if four conditions are met the High Court must transfer the application to the Upper Tribunal.

---

[20]    Tribunals, Courts and Enforcement Act 2007, s 19(1).

4.74    The conditions are:

    (1)    that the application does not seek anything other than a quashing, prohibiting or mandatory order, a declaration, such damages as are available in judicial review (including interest), and costs;

    (2)    that the application does not call into question anything done by the Crown Court;

    (3)    that the application falls within a class over which the Upper Tribunal has jurisdiction under section 18(6) of the Tribunals, Courts and Enforcement Act 2007; and

    (4)    that the application does not call into question any decision made under the Immigration Acts, the British Nationality Act 1981, instruments made under these or a question of citizenship.

4.75    In opting for a model based on the transfer of a case to the ombudsmen, we wish to highlight that it would still be possible for an ombudsman subsequently to abandon an investigation – or to resort to a reporting mechanism of a lesser nature than a full report. The mechanisms available to the public services ombudsmen are considered in greater detail in the next two Parts. A decision to take such action would, of course, be amenable to judicial review.

4.76    Given the responses to consultation, **we provisionally propose that there should be a stay and transfer power allowing matters to be transferred from the courts to the public services ombudsmen.**

4.77    **Do consultees agree that the court should invite submissions from the original parties before transferring the matter?**

4.78    **Do consultees agree that, in the event of such a transfer, the ombudsman should be obliged to open an investigation?**

4.79    **Do consultees agree that the ombudsman should also be able to abandon the investigation should it – in their opinion – not disclose maladministration?**

**Alternatives to investigation**

4.80    The previous sections considered very formal alternatives to ombudsmen, such as courts or tribunals. Here we wish to highlight a provision in the most recent of the governing statutes for the public services ombudsmen. Section 3 of the Public Services Ombudsman (Wales) Act 2005 allows the ombudsman to use such alternative methods to investigate as it sees fit. These can be either in addition or as an alternative to investigation. These must be conducted in private.[21]

4.81    In 2009-2010, the annual report of the Public Services Ombudsman for Wales listed the number of complaints resolved voluntarily – including those referred to as "quick fix" cases – which amounted to 90 complaints. This was out of the 482

---

[21]    Public Services Ombudsman (Wales) Act 2005, s 3(2).

complaints made which were neither "not investigated" nor "withdrawn". This comes to 19 per cent.[22]

4.82 There is no similar power in the Parliamentary Commissioner Act 1967, which is hardly surprising given its pedigree, or for the Health Service Ombudsman and the Local Government Ombudsman. There are, however, provisions for the Parliamentary Commissioner and the Local Government Ombudsman relating to the appointment of mediators to assist in the conduct of an investigation.[23] However, these powers are not drawn as widely as that in section 3 of the Public Services Ombudsman (Wales) Act 2005 and do not provide a potential alternative to opening an investigation.

4.83 Paragraph 2(1)(a) of schedule 2 of the Housing Act 1996 means that the Secretary of State can only approve an ombudsman scheme if it contains "a power of the Housing Ombudsman to propose alternative methods of resolving a dispute". On this basis, we do not think it necessary to make provisional proposals in relation to the Housing Ombudsman.

4.84 We consider a power to use alternative dispute mechanisms to be useful and appropriate in these circumstances, especially considering the expanding role of alternative dispute resolution in other contexts – particularly that of the Administrative Court.[24] We do not see any point in limiting the availability of alternative dispute resolution. Therefore, we have a preference in favour of the more broadly drawn power in section 3 of the Public Services Ombudsman (Wales) Act 2005.

4.85 **We provisionally propose that the Parliamentary Commissioner, the Local Government Ombudsman and the Health Service Ombudsman be given specific powers to allow them to dispose of complaints in ways other than by conducting an investigation.**

## FORMAL REQUIREMENTS

### Written complaints

4.86 Here we consider whether a complaint should be written. This is important as a requirement for a complaint to be written potentially disenfranchises certain individuals, particularly those who are uncomfortable with writing or whose first language is not English.

4.87 The governing statutes contain a variety of approaches to the requirement that a complaint be written. Under section 5(1)(a) of the Parliamentary Commissioner Act 1967, a complaint must be written. There is no discretion as to this requirement. Under section 9(2) of the Health Service Commissioners Act 1993,

---

[22] Public Services Ombudsman for Wales, *Annual Report 2009-10* (2010) p 15.

[23] Parliamentary Commissioner Act 1967, s 3(1A) and Local Government Act 1974, s 29(6A), inserted by the Regulatory Reform (Collaboration etc between Ombudsmen) Order 2007 SI 2007 No 1889, art 12.

[24] *Cowl v Plymouth City Council* [2001] EWCA Civ 1935, [2002] 1 WLR 803. S Boyron, "The rise in mediation in administrative law disputes: experiences from England, France and Germany" [2006] *Public Law* 320. For research on the effects of this, see V Bondy and L Mulcahy, *Mediation and judicial review: an empirical research study* (2009).

a complaint must be in writing and there is no discretion. The Health Service Ombudsman is, therefore, in the same position as the Parliamentary Commissioner.

4.88 Section 5(1)(a) of the Public Services Ombudsman (Wales) Act 2005 contains a formal requirement that a complaint be in writing. However, in opening a complaint, under section 2(4) the ombudsman can investigate a matter even if the requirements of section 5(1) are not met, if it thinks it reasonable to do so.

4.89 Section 26B of the Local Government Act 1974 was inserted by the Local Government and Public Involvement in Health Act 2007. Section 26B(1)(a) requires that a complaint should be made in writing. However, in section 26B(3) there is a discretion to wave the formal requirements for particular complaints. In the original section 26 of the Local Government Act 1974 there was a formal requirement that a complaint be made in writing, with no discretion.

4.90 There are no requirements in schedule 2 of the Housing Act 1996 except that a complaint should be duly made. Neither are there any requirements as to form in the approved scheme document for the Independent Housing Ombudsman Scheme. We do not want to create exclusionary hurdles where there are none at present. Therefore, we are not making any provisional proposals in relation to the Housing Ombudsman.

4.91 We provisionally consider that the provisions in the Parliamentary Commissioner Act 1967 and the Health Service Commissioners Act 1993 are unacceptable in modern terms. **We provisionally propose that a discretionary provision relating to formal requirements, similar to section 26B(3) of the Local Government Act 1974, be inserted into the governing statutes for the Parliamentary Commissioner and the Health Service Ombudsman, excluding the Housing Ombudsman. This would allow them to dispense with the requirement that a complaint be in writing.**

**MP filter**

4.92 The MP filter is unique to the Parliamentary Commissioner. Section 5 of the Parliamentary Commissioner Act 1967 requires that a complaint should be "duly made to a Member of the House of Commons" who can then refer it to the Parliamentary Commissioner.

*Our consultation paper*

4.93 In our consultation paper *Administrative Redress: Public Bodies and the Citizen* we proposed two options for reform – either abolition or a dual track:

> Do consultees consider that the filter should be abolished outright, or that there should be a "dual system" which would allow complainants the option of making a complaint through an MP or of seeking direct access to the Parliamentary Ombudsman?[25]

We consider the consultation responses to the reform of the MP filter in the context of these options.

---

[25] CP 187, para 5.88.

37

ABOLITION

4.94 Thirty-two consultees responded on the first issue, and all but one was in agreement with the proposal to abolish the MP filter in its present form.

4.95 Whilst strong support was expressed in many responses, reasons given by consultees largely reiterated the points made in the consultation paper.

4.96 The Public Administration Select Committee said:

> We have long recommended the abolition of the MP filter, as it has been shown to be a barrier to access to the Parliamentary Ombudsman service. A clear majority of MPs favoured the abolition of the filter in summer 2004, according to the results of a survey that we and the [Parliamentary and Health Service Ombudsman] conducted jointly at the time.

DUAL-TRACK SYSTEM

4.97 Twenty-four responses considered the alternatives. Sixteen consultees preferred a dual system, eight favoured outright abolition. By dual-track system, we meant that individuals would have direct access to the Parliamentary Commissioner. However, it would still be possible for Members of Parliament to forward complaints to the Parliamentary Commissioner where they thought this appropriate.

4.98 Several consultees preferred a dual system because it recognised the importance of the relationship between Parliament and the Parliamentary Commissioner for Administration. The Parliamentary and Health Service Ombudsman suggested that the MP filter was "an acknowledgement of [the] close constitutional relationship" between the Parliamentary Commissioner and Parliament.

4.99 The Public Administration Select Committee agreed. It stated that the Parliamentary Commissioner was reliant on Members of Parliament to apply political pressure to the Government, so the maintenance of a close working relationship was important. The committee also noted that the dual track system might usefully be extended to the Health Service Ombudsman.

4.100 Several consultees argued that if the MP filter were removed entirely then a system of notification should be put in its place. This would preserve the close relationship between the Parliamentary Commissioner and Parliament. Professor Colin Reid favoured the "outright abolition of the MP filter", but added two conditions that in appearance resemble a dual system:

> a) a requirement on the ombudsman to notify MPs of non-frivolous complaints received and b) the potential for MPs to refer cases to the ombudsman (with the complainant's permission).

4.101 A number of consultees did not see the need for a dual system. Participants at the Advice Services Alliance seminar pointed out that there is already provision for a third party (including an MP) to make a complaint on behalf of another person.

### Conclusions

4.102 Considering our consultation responses, the Collcutt review[26] and the position of the Public Administration Select Committee,[27] there seems to be a clear movement in favour of reforming the MP filter. There does not seem to be any valid argument in favour of retaining an exclusionary bar to the opening of an investigation by the Parliamentary Commissioner. However, there are differences in opinion as to how the MP filter should be reformed. For instance, Collcutt favoured outright abolition whereas the current Parliamentary Commissioner prefers the dual-track system.

4.103 We are persuaded that there is value in maintaining a direct link with individual Members of Parliament. We have already shown, in Part 2, that we think Parliament should have a greater role in the appointment of the public services ombudsmen. In Parts 6 and 7 we consider other ways in which the relationship between the public services ombudsmen and Parliament can be strengthened.

4.104 Given that outright abolition could be seen as symbolically ending the direct relationship between individual Members and the Parliamentary Commissioner, we suggest that the dual-track approach is preferable to outright abolition. This allows for specific provision to be made for the continuing involvement of a Member who referred a complaint to the Parliamentary Commissioner. This is potentially of especial importance where a report is issued.

4.105 A potential model could be taken from the Local Government Act 1974, as reformed. Though it is not necessary for a complaint to come from a councillor, there is still the ability – under section 26C of the Local Government Act 1974 – for members of an authority to forward complaints to the ombudsman, with the consent of the initial complainant.

4.106 Therefore, **we provisionally propose that a dual-track approach to reform of the MP filter be adopted by Parliament.**

---

[26] Cabinet Office, *Review of the public sector ombudsmen in England* (2000). This recommended the abolition of the MP filter at para 3.52.

[27] Parliament and the Ombudsman, Report of the Public Administration Select Committee (2009-10) HC 107, para 6 recommended the abolition of the MP filter. Also, Parliament and the Ombudsman: Further Report, Report of the Public Administration Select Committee (2009-10) HC 471, para 3.

# PART 5
# OMBUDSMEN INVESTIGATIONS

## INTRODUCTION

5.1 There are special features of the ombudsmen that mark them as different from other mechanisms of administrative redress. This Part considers the process adopted, or which should be adopted, by the public services ombudsmen.

5.2 In doing this we focus on a particular aspect of the current process – its closed nature. In earlier consultation events, the issue of joint working with regulators was raised. It appears that, since our original consultation, practices for joint working have developed of their own accord. Therefore, we have decided that there is no need to pursue this issue any further.

5.3 We also return to a tool that we provisionally proposed in our consultation paper *Administrative Redress: Public Bodies and the Citizen*. This is the possibility of the ombudsmen referring a question on a point of law to a court.

## CLOSED NATURE OF OMBUDSMEN INVESTIGATIONS

5.4 The ombudsman process is investigatory. Describing ombudsmen in general, the International Bar Association considered the "power to investigate" was part of the definition of an ombudsman,[1] as did a 1991 UK conference on ombudsmen.[2]

5.5 The original vision for ombudsmen investigations was that they should be "conducted as informally as possible".[3] Though there are powers to call witnesses, a large part of the investigatory process is paper based.[4]

5.6 One particular feature that we wish to explore is the closed, confidential nature of ombudsmen investigations. The effect of this, in terms of the process, is that there is no general, publically available information as to investigations underway. This can be contrasted with the procedure for courts, which are normally in the open. Tribunals are also mostly conducted in the open. However, there are exceptions to the general rule such as the Health, Education and Social Care Chamber of the First-tier Tribunal.

5.7 A further feature considered in the next Part of this consultation paper is that the identity of the complainant is not disclosed – even where a report on maladministration is issued.

---

[1] Quoted in W Haller, "The place of the ombudsman in the world community" (1988) *Fourth international ombudsman conference papers* 29. Referred to in M Seneviratne, *Ombudsmen: Public service and administrative justice* (2002) p 8.

[2] M Hayes, "Emerging issues for ombudsmen" (1991) *UK ombudsmen conference paper* 5. Referred to in M Seneviratne, *Ombudsmen: Public service and administrative justice* (2002) p 25.

[3] *Hansard* (HC), 18 October 1966, vol 734, col 45.

[4] If necessary, the ombudsmen have broad powers to obtain access to administrative records: M Seneviratne, *Ombudsmen: Public service and administrative justice* (2002) p 119.

**Statutory provisions**

5.8 There is a general requirement that public services ombudsmen's investigations must be conducted in private. This is true for the governing statutes of all the public services ombudsmen, except the Housing Ombudsman.[5] Unusually, both the Housing Act 1996 and the governing document for the Independent Housing Ombudsman Scheme are silent as to any requirements for privacy.

5.9 This formal requirement contrasts with the flexibility that the ombudsmen are normally accorded in the conduct of their inquiries. So, for instance, under section 13(3) of the Public Services Ombudsman (Wales) Act 2005, "the procedure for conducting an investigation is to be such as the ombudsman thinks appropriate in the circumstances of the case". Similar provisions occur in the governing statutes for the Parliamentary Commissioner,[6] the Health Service Ombudsman[7] and the Local Government Ombudsman.[8]

5.10 There are limited statutory exceptions within the governing statutes for the public services ombudsmen, which make provision for the sharing of information. These are to allow for joint working with other ombudsmen,[9] other regulators[10] and the work of the Information Commissioner.[11]

5.11 Two further exceptions to the general rule against non-disclosure are relevant. The Health Service Ombudsman can disclose information "to any persons to whom he thinks it should be disclosed in the interests of the health and safety of patients".[12] This power may be used where a complaint has been made and the investigation reveals activity that should be brought to the attention of the General Medical Council or a similar disciplinary body. A more widely drawn power was given to the Public Services Ombudsman for Wales who "in the case of information to the effect that a person is likely to constitute a threat to the health or safety of one or more persons" can disclose such information "to any person to whom the ombudsman thinks it should be disclosed in the public interest".[13] This reflects the wider jurisdiction of the Public Services Ombudsman for Wales. It includes not only the health service but also matters such as adult social care, where those who may need protection could not be classified as a patient.

---

[5] See: Public Services Ombudsman (Wales) Act, s 13(2); Parliamentary Commissioner Act 1967, s 7(2); Health Service Commissioners Act 1993, s 11(2); Local Government Act 1974, s 28(2).

[6] Parliamentary Commissioner Act 1967, s 7(2).

[7] Health Service Commissioners Act 1993, s 11(3).

[8] Local Government Act 1974, s 28(2).

[9] See: Public Services Ombudsman (Wales) Act, s 25; Parliamentary Commissioner Act 1967, ss 11A and 11ZAA; Health Service Commissioners Act 1993, s 11(3); Local Government Act 1974, ss 33 and 33ZA.

[10] Public Services Ombudsman (Wales) Act, ss 25A and 25B.

[11] See: Public Services Ombudsman (Wales) Act, ss 26(3) to (5); Parliamentary Commissioner Act 1967, s 11AA; Health Service Commissioners Act 1993, s 11(3); Local Government Act 1974, s 33A.

[12] Health Service Commissioners Act 1993, ss 15(1)(e) and 15(1B).

[13] Public Services Ombudsman (Wales) Act, s 26(2)(i).

5.12 There is no general power to disclose information to the general public. The above provisions merely provide for specific, and limited, circumstances where the general rule may be disapplied.

**Arguments in favour of the closed approach to ombudsmen investigations**

5.13 There is an argument that the closed nature of the process protects the ombudsmen's flexibility in choosing their investigatory technique. If the process were exposed to general public scrutiny then this would risk over-formalisation and reduce the ombudsmen's ability to react to the individual circumstances of a case.

5.14 The closed nature of investigations also reduces the risks to the reputation of the public body in cases where the complaint is subsequently found to be unsubstantiated.

5.15 Finally, it is arguably the case that the closed nature of the process makes it more likely that the public bodies being investigated will share documentation. This would prevent ombudsmen needing recourse to their broad powers to compel release.

**Conclusions and provisional proposals for reform**

5.16 We are aware how important this issue is to the public services ombudsmen. However, we are also aware that the law relating to openness and transparency has changed dramatically since the drafting and passing of the first statute in 1967, which has been recreated in similar terms in all the subsequent statutes bar that for the Housing Ombudsman. The closed nature of the Whitehall process in 1967 would be unacceptable in the context of the current landscape of public law.

5.17 We think it is interesting that the basic approach in the original statute for the Parliamentary Commissioner has been adopted in all subsequent statutes – though with limited alterations – including the most recent, the Public Services Ombudsman (Wales) Act 2005. However, we do not think that this precludes reform.

5.18 The closed nature of ombudsmen investigations does not necessarily fit with modern requirements for public administration. The default position should be that the business of public bodies is conducted in a transparent manner. This is the normal position for courts and many tribunals. Closed investigations mean that the methodology adopted by the public services ombudsmen in their investigations is harder to scrutinise. This can lead some to query the independence of the public services ombudsmen from those they are tasked to investigate.

5.19 However, the need for transparency is not absolute and there are possible benefits to the current process that – as set out in the preceding section – potentially mitigate against investigations being exposed to public scrutiny in all circumstances.

5.20 We suggest that there is a balance between the modern preferences for transparency and the efficient, informal operation of ombudsmen investigations.

We suggest there may be times when revealing the nature of the complaint would jeopardise the completion of an investigation.

5.21   Our provisional conclusion is that, given the modern development of transparency as administrative preference, the current prohibition on openness except in certain statutorily defined circumstances in unsustainable.

5.22   We do not think that it would be appropriate to suggest that all investigations be open. Given how important the closed nature is seen to be for the core investigatory process of the public services ombudsmen, we think that the vast majority of investigations would still be conducted in private.

5.23   We think it should be for the ombudsmen to develop a system such that they release suitable information to the general public.

5.24   Our aim is to give the ombudsmen greater control over disclosure, rather than to suggest what should or should not be disclosed. However, we see that there is a good case in general for the disclosure of, for instance, the identity of public bodies subject to investigation and the service area concerned. It may also be helpful to have the power to identify a complainant with their consent.

5.25   There is a significant issue in relation to the Freedom of Information Act 2000. The public services ombudsmen, except the Housing Ombudsman, are bodies listed in schedule 1 of the Freedom of Information Act 2000. They are, therefore, subject to its provisions and – most importantly – the general right of access to information contained in section 1 of that Act. Under their governing statutes, ombudsmen investigations are to be conducted in private and the information only distributed in limited circumstances. Consequently, such information as relates to the investigation falls within section 44(1). This grants an absolute exemption to the section 1 right where publication is prohibited by statute.

5.26   The creation of a more general power to release information during investigations would mean that the public services ombudsmen would lose the absolute exemption available to them in section 44(1) of the Freedom of Information Act 2000.

5.27   Our general strategy is to allow the ombudsmen wider powers relating to disclosure, not to impose additional burdens on them. Whilst the Freedom of Information Act 2000 is a valuable mechanism that encourages transparent government, the duty to disclose is not absolute and was never meant to be.

5.28   Documents used in an investigation would arguably still fall within section 22 of the Freedom of Information Act 2000. This grants an exemption for information intended for future publication. Personal information would remain exempt under section 40, as would material provided in confidence under section 41 of the Freedom of Information Act 2000.

5.29   In order to avoid creating additional burdens, whilst still granting the ombudsmen the freedom to release information, we suggest that it may be necessary for there to be specific exemptions from section 1 of the Freedom of Information Act 2000 for investigations by the public services ombudsmen. These could be placed in the existing statutes governing the ombudsmen. The legal position in relation to the duty to disclose in section 1 of the Freedom of Information Act 2000 would therefore remain the same as is currently the case.

5.30 A different option would be to give the other public services ombudsmen a similar power to that held by the Public Services Ombudsman for Wales. Under section 36(5)(ka) of the Freedom of Information Act 2000, he can decide that certain information should not be disclosed if such disclosure would "prejudice the effective conduct of public affairs". This acts as a qualified exemption to the section 1 duty. So, the ombudsman needs to consider whether such prejudice would take place. This decision needs to be communicated to the individual citizen.

5.31 Section 36(5)(ka) of the Freedom of Information Act 2000 is narrower in its scope than the more general bar that currently exists. Therefore, pursuing this as a model would still lead to the creation of additional burdens on the ombudsmen.

5.32 Given the quasi-judicial nature of the work of the ombudsmen, we suggest that of the two options set out above, the creation of a new absolute exemption for information relating to investigations would be more appropriate. The effect of our provisional proposal would therefore be to encourage and allow for transparency during investigations without imposing it.

5.33 **We provisionally propose that there should be statutory discretion for the public services ombudsmen to dispense with the requirement that an investigation be conducted in private in situations where they see this as appropriate.**

5.34 **Do consultees think that, if such discretion were created, the public services ombudsmen should be protected from additional burdens?**

5.35 **If so, would consultees prefer a more general exemption from the duty contained in section 1 of the Freedom of Information Act 2000 in relation to investigations, as is currently the case? Alternatively, would consultees prefer a more limited exemption modelled on section 36(5)(ka) of the Freedom of Information Act 2000?**

**REFERENCE ON A POINT OF LAW**

5.36 In our consultation paper *Administrative Redress: Public Bodies and the Citizen* we provisionally proposed that the public services ombudsmen be given a power to refer a question to a court on a point of law.[14] In doing this, we suggested that the ombudsmen should consider the following factors before making a reference:

(1) The ombudsman must consider that the determination of the particular legal question is necessary for it to make a finding of maladministration.

(2) A legal question should only be referred if it is contentious or unresolved. If it has already been determined or is pending determination by the courts, a reference will be unnecessary.

---

[14] CP 187, paras 5.43 to 5.46.

(3)   A reference should not be made where it is more appropriate for the whole dispute to be dealt with by a court. The reference procedure should be invoked only where the complaint is essentially about maladministration but cannot be progressed without prior resolution of a legal issue.[15]

### Consultation responses

5.37   In our consultation paper *Administrative Redress: Public Bodies and the Citizen* we asked two questions relating to the introduction of a reference procedure for ombudsmen.

SHOULD THERE BE A POWER TO MAKE A REFERENCE?

5.38   First, we asked whether "consultees think that the ombudsmen should have the power to make references to the court of points of law".[16] Twenty-eight consultees supported this proposal, one did not.

5.39   Two consultees drew attention to the territorial remit of the Parliamentary Commissioner for Administration, and queried what effect allowing references on a point of law would have on this. Professor Colin Reid wondered whether the Parliamentary Commissioner would be able to refer a complaint brought by a Scottish individual against HM Revenue and Customs to a court in England. The Parliamentary and Health Service Ombudsman suggested that the Parliamentary Commissioner would have to "engage with those responsible for the administration of the courts in Northern Ireland and Scotland".

5.40   Several consultees raised concerns as to how the reference procedure would work in practice – particularly with relation to the costs of the process. Mr Justice Silber suggested that a process similar to the case stated procedure could be used.

5.41   The Public Law Project cautioned that the ability of the parties to be able to have an input into the proceedings would need to be considered. This would also raise questions of funding "given the usually greater resources available to defendants compared with claimants". However, York Law School suggested that:

> While the public sector body should if they wish to oppose the application fund their own costs, the normal outcome of such an application would be no costs order.

5.42   At a seminar organised by the Advice Services Alliance, participants raised several issues about the reference process: the circumstances in which the ombudsman would decide that a reference is or is not necessary; who would draft the reference and how; how the court would decide the point of law; what would be the status of the court's decision; the likelihood of an increase of judicial review claims against the ombudsman; and costs.

5.43   Zurich Financial Services disagreed with the proposal altogether on the grounds that it would result in arguments of law requiring legal representation. Zurich felt

[15]  CP 187, para 5.46.

[16]  CP 187, para 5.47.

that this would take any reference "outside the ombudsman remit". Conversely, the Administrative Justice and Tribunals Council argued that a reference power would "complement the ombudsmen's functions and utility without compromising their non-judicial role".

5.44 The second question we asked in the *Administrative Redress* consultation paper was:

> Do consultees think that references from the ombudsmen should bypass the permission stage before proceeding to the Administrative Court?[17]

5.45 Twenty responses discussed this issue. Fourteen consultees were in favour of the proposal for references to bypass permission; six were against it.

5.46 The Parliamentary and Health Service Ombudsman felt that it was essential that the permission stage should be bypassed in the interests of preventing delay. Tom Hickman agreed, as a permission stage would result in further issues as to representation of the parties and costs. Mr Justice Sullivan saw no need for a permission stage because:

> The procedure would be more akin to an appeal by case stated. Once the case has been stated by the decision taker, there is no need to obtain the Court's permission to pursue the appeal.

5.47 The Local Government Ombudsman suggested that there could be periodic reviews between the Administrative Court and ombudsmen. This would ensure that the system was working smoothly without a permission stage.

5.48 However, Mr Justice Silber felt strongly that it was essential for the Administrative Court to exercise control over references through a permission stage. He argued that without it there was a risk that ombudsmen who were not lawyers might refer "inappropriate questions or ill-defined issues or hopeless applications". The permission stage would therefore allow the Administrative Court judge a chance to seek clarification or amendment of the reference.

### Further investigation and potential models

5.49 The general response from our consultation on references on points of law was positive. There was widespread agreement that a reference procedure could provide a necessary and useful tool for ombudsmen. We do not agree with the argument put forward by Zurich Financial Services that a court-based reference procedure would take ombudsmen outside of their non-legal remit. To the contrary, allowing ombudsmen to refer questions of law to a court would enable them to focus their investigations exclusively on facts and questions of maladministration.

5.50 We agree with the majority of consultees who felt that the reference procedure should bypass the permission stage of the Administrative Court. Any reference

---

[17] CP 187, para 5.53.

procedure will only have value if it contributes to the efficient resolution of ombudsmen investigations. Therefore, the potential for delay in going through the permission stage would be inappropriate.

5.51 However, the responses from our consultation did highlight the practical difficulties of implementing a reference procedure. There are two key considerations that must be borne in mind when attempting to construct a procedure for references on a point of law:

(1) The need for all parties to be able to make representations to the Administrative Court regarding the reference.

(2) The need to avoid complainants having to incur significant costs. This would undermine one of the key strengths of the ombudsman process and could potentially create an imbalance between public bodies and individual complainants (particularly as complainants will be unlikely to qualify for legal aid).

5.52 In attempting to meet these key concerns we have considered a number of existing reference procedures as potential models on which a reference procedure could be based. We will give a brief summary of these other procedures below.

### Preliminary rulings on European Union law

5.53 Under article 267 of the Treaty on the Functioning of the European Union, national courts may refer questions of European Union law to the Court of Justice of the European Union where an answer is "necessary to enable [them] to give judgment".[18]

5.54 National courts have the primary responsibility for applying European Union norms and the application of a ruling to the facts of any case falls exclusively to them. Thus, the relationship between the Court of Justice and domestic courts of member states is co-operative rather than hierarchical. This equal relationship is reinforced by the fact that the Court of Justice only has the power to give a preliminary ruling – which is in the nature of an interlocutory reference, not an appeal.[19]

5.55 The question which forms the reference is submitted by the court of a member state. Other member states, the European Commission, the original parties to the case and, in some circumstances, other institutions of the European Union are then notified. All those who are notified are entitled to submit written observations to the Court of Justice. There is also a chance to intervene at a subsequent hearing.[20]

---

[18] Treaty on the Functioning of the European Union, art 267; formerly Treaty Establishing the European Community, art 234.

[19] See *Information note on references from national courts for a preliminary ruling* Official Journal C 297 of 5.12.2009 p 1, paras 5 and 7.

[20] See Statute of the European Court of Justice, art 23 and Rules of Procedure of the European Court of Justice, Official Journal C 177 of 2.7.2010 p 1, arts 103 to 104.

5.56    The Court of Justice of the European Union's rules of procedure state that, in considering the representation at the preliminary ruling of individual parties to the dispute, the Court shall:

> Take account of the rules of procedure of the national court or tribunal which made the reference.[21]

5.57    Regarding costs, these are determined at a national level:

> Proceedings for a preliminary ruling before the Court are free of charge and the Court does not rule on the costs of the parties to the main proceedings; it is for the national court to rule on those costs.

> If a party has insufficient means and where possible under national rules, the national court may grant that party legal aid to cover the costs, including those of lawyers' fees, which it incurs before the Court. The Court itself may also grant legal aid.[22]

### *Appeals by way of case stated*

5.58    There are numerous statutes which provide for a right of appeal by way of case stated to a higher court, against a decision of a lower court or tribunal, or another public authority. For example, decisions of magistrates' courts and those of the Crown Court that do not relate to trial on indictment[23] can be appealed to the High Court.

5.59    So, for instance, the alleged failure of a magistrates' court to enforce an abatement notice issued under section 80 of the Environment Protection Act 1990 can be challenged by way of case stated under section 111(1) of Magistrates' Court Act 1980.[24]

5.60    Where an appeal is made against an enforcement notice issued under Part VII of the Town and Country Planning Act 1992, in the course of that appeal the Secretary of State "may state any question of law arising in the course of the proceedings in the form of a special case for the decision of the High Court".[25] The decision of the High Court on such a question is considered a judgment of the Court for the purposes of section 16 of the Senior Courts Act 1981. It can, therefore, be subject to appeal to the Court of Appeal.[26]

5.61    When a reference is made in this way (without the request of either of the parties) the Secretary of State must serve the stated case on all parties that he or she

---

[21]    Rules of Procedure of the Court of Justice, Official Journal C 177 of 2.7.2010 p 1, art 104(2).

[22]    *Information note on references from national courts for a preliminary ruling* Official Journal C 297 of 5.12.2009 p 1, paras 27 to 28.

[23]    Magistrates' Court Act 1980, s 111(1); Senior Courts Act 1981, s 28.

[24]    *St Albans District Council v Patel* [2008] EWHC 2767 (Admin), [2009] Env LR 22.

[25]    Town and Country Planning Act 1990, s 289(3).

[26]    Town and Country Planning Act 1990, s 289(4).

considers appropriate and give notice to the parties that the case has been served.[27]

### Devolution issues

5.62    The statutes governing devolution[28] give the relevant officers of the devolved administrations the power to make references to the Supreme Court – formerly to the Judicial Committee of the Privy Council – on "devolution issues".[29]

5.63    Of the different ways in which this can happen, potentially relevant for our purposes is where a relevant officer can ask a question of the Supreme Court concerning the jurisdiction of the institutions of the devolved administrations.[30] Section 33(1) of the Scotland Act 1998 – to take an example – provides that:

> The Advocate General, the Lord Advocate or the Attorney General may refer the question of whether a Bill or any provision of a Bill would be within the legislative competence of the Parliament to the Supreme Court for decision.

5.64    Practice Direction 10 of the Supreme Court is silent as to other parties, excepting the requirement that the other relevant officers for that jurisdiction should be informed and have the ability to intervene. To stay with the Scottish example, this means that the Attorney General and the Advocate General for Scotland should be informed if the Lord Advocate is making the reference.

5.65    To our knowledge this power or the similar powers for Wales and Northern Ireland have never been used. What it does show is that such a single actor, non-adversarial, reference power does exist in modern statutes, and was envisaged to be useful for questions of jurisdiction.

### Advisory opinions of the Judicial Committee of the Privy Council

5.66    The devolution jurisdiction considered above is distinct from the more general advisory jurisdiction that the Judicial Committee of the Privy Council has under section 4 of the Judicial Committee Act 1833.

5.67    The most recent example of this power being used was in 2009, where the Privy Council had to consider the circumstances in which the Chief Justice for Gibraltar could be removed from office.[31] The Gibraltar Constitution Order 2006 states that the Chief Justice can be removed by the Governor after Her Majesty has sought the advice of the Judicial Committee of the Privy Council under section 4 of the Judicial Committee Act 1833. Neither the rules of the Judicial Committee nor Practice Directions set out a specific procedure for this. In *re Chief Justice on*

---

[27]    Civil Procedure Rules, Practice Direction 52, para 18.9.

[28]    Scotland Act 1998, Northern Ireland Act 1998, Government of Wales Act 2006.

[29]    Depending on the jurisdiction from which the case arises, the relevant officers may be: the Lord Advocate; Advocate General for Scotland; Attorney General for Northern Ireland; Advocate General for Northern Ireland; Counsel General for the Welsh Assembly Government; and, the Attorney General. See Supreme Court Rules 2009, r 3.

[30]    See: Scotland Act 1998, s 33; Northern Ireland Act 1998, s 11; Government of Wales Act 2006, ss 96, 99 and 112.

[31]    *Re Chief Justice of Gibraltar* [2009] UKPC 43.

*Gibraltar* separate counsel were instructed by the Chief Justice, the Governor General of Gibraltar and the Government of Gibraltar.

5.68    In *Re Parliamentary Privilege Act 1770*, a simple question was put before the Judicial Committee. The Attorney General argued for an affirmative answer, whilst the Treasury Solicitor argued for a negative one. The party potentially affected by the result intervened.[32]

5.69    Though the opinion is not binding, it is usually followed.

### References by the Attorney General

5.70    Under section 36 of the Criminal Justice Act 1972 the Attorney General may make a referral, "if he desires the opinion of the Court of Appeal on a point of law which has arisen" in the case of a person acquitted of an offence under indictment.[33]

5.71    The reference to the court is in writing and must specify the point of law at issue and the facts of the case, where this is appropriate. The registrar of the court ensures that a copy of the reference is served upon the person acquitted.[34] The acquitted person may be represented, or a defence petition may be represented by the appointment of a friend of the court.

### Conclusions and provisional proposals

5.72    The above examples all demonstrate the various ways in which courts may receive requests to clarify areas of legal uncertainty. However, we are not convinced that any of them provides a wholly suitable model for an ombudsman reference procedure.

5.73    All of the mechanisms considered above involve going before a court. However, that may not be necessary in all circumstances. In order to reduce the potential burdens on courts and the ombudsmen that this would entail, it may be best to take alternative action before resorting to the courts.

5.74    We suggest that the public services ombudsmen should be able to seek the opinion of counsel before making a reference to a court on a point of law. There seem to us two ways in which this could be carried out. First, the public services ombudsmen could be given the equivalent of a "QC clause" such as exists in certain insurance agreements. This could be done by inserting into the Civil Procedure Rules, or incorporating within a Practice Direction, a requirement to seek the opinion of counsel, save in the circumstances set out in paragraph 5.76 below.

5.75    Alternatively, seeking the advice of a QC could be seen as a specific form of arbitration and be governed by the Arbitration Act 1996 and Part 62 of the Civil Procedure Rules. In this case, we suggest that parties should be asked whether they agree to arbitration by an arbitral tribunal consisting of a single counsel

---

[32]    *Re Parliamentary Privilege Act 1770* [1958] AC 331.

[33]    Criminal Justice Act 1972, s 36.

[34]    Criminal Procedure Rules 2005, SI 2005 No 384, paras 69.1 and 69.2.

recommended by the public services ombudsman. If agreement is reached, then there should be no need to make a reference. If agreement cannot be reached then a reference can still be made by the public services ombudsman. This option has the disadvantage that it would be considerably more costly than the "QC Clause" approach and may even cost the same as a reference.

5.76    We are aware that the public services ombudsmen, and on occasions the complainant and public body complained against, already seek advice from counsel. In circumstances where the parties have already sought the advice of leading counsel it may not make sense for a further opinion to be sought which could add to divergent opinions. Consequently it may be that an imperative to seek counsel's advice before making a reference to the court is not necessary. Therefore, we ask an open question on the issue.

5.77    Costs of counsel, which may be as arbitrator's fees, should be met by the public services ombudsman.

5.78    One issue has surfaced in all of the discussions we have had on a possible reference procedure. This concerns the problem of creating a viable court-based mechanism which originates in a non-adversarial process. To the best of our knowledge, the examples we gave of such mechanisms, devolution references and section 289(3) of the Town and Country Planning Act 1990, have never been used.

5.79    In relation to representation, we suggest that there are – broadly – two options. First, the ombudsman could instruct a single counsel to put both sides of the question to the court. This has advantages in terms of efficiency and cost. The alternative would be for the ombudsman to instruct two counsel, with each representing different sides of the question. This would suit the adversarial nature of the courts in England and Wales. We also suggest that this would improve the quality of the decision, and be more acceptable to the judiciary. We can see benefits to both options, hence we ask an open consultation question rather than make provisional proposals below.

5.80    A distinct but related issue is the extent to which interested parties may intervene. We think that it would be appropriate to allow intervention by interested parties subject to the normal case management powers of the court.

5.81    There is one further issue in allowing interventions. The current ombudsman process is based around the privacy of the complainant. The complainant may see it as problematic to intervene before a court whose default position is openness. The alternatives would seem to be to allow anonymous intervention or to require a complainant to relinquish anonymity if they sought to intervene.

5.82    Initial indications from the ombudsmen are that a reference procedure would be used mainly to determine questions of jurisdiction. This leads to our present formulation of the referral procedure. We see it primarily as a mechanism to allow an ombudsman to make a reference in order to avoid straying out of their jurisdiction and leaving themselves potentially susceptible to the judicial review of a report.

*Pre-reference*

5.83    Before making a reference to a court on a point of law, should there be a requirement that the public services ombudsmen seek either the opinion of or arbitration by an independent counsel?

5.84    We provisionally propose that the counsel's fees should be met by the public services ombudsmen.

*Basic procedure for a reference to a court of law*

5.85    We provisionally propose that the there should be a mechanism allowing a public services ombudsman to ask a question of the Administrative Court.

5.86    We provisionally propose that such a reference should not require permission.

5.87    We provisionally propose that the decision of the Administrative Court on such a matter should be considered a judgment of the Court for the purposes of section 16 of the Senior Courts Act 1981 and, therefore, potentially subject to appeal to the Court of Appeal.

*The decision to refer*

5.88    We provisionally propose that the public services ombudsmen should notify the complainant and the relevant public bodies of their intention to make a referral on a point of law, invite them to submit their views and/or to intervene before the court should they wish to.

5.89    We provisionally propose that the final decision whether to refer a question to the court should be solely that for the public services ombudsman.

*Parties to the action*

5.90    Should the ombudsman routinely instruct one counsel to put both sides of the question or should two opposing counsel be instructed?

5.91    We provisionally propose that other interested parties may intervene, subject to case management decisions of the court.

*Costs*

5.92    We provisionally propose that, subject to the use of costs orders for case management purposes, the default position should be all parties or interveners – including the public services ombudsmen – should meet their own costs.

# PART 6
# REPORTING

## INTRODUCTION

6.1 This Part considers the final stage of the ombudsman process - reporting the results of an investigation. This includes the communication of a decision not to open an investigation or to abandon an existing one. We also consider wider powers allowing the ombudsmen to issue reports on more general matters, such as principles of good administrative practice.

6.2 This Part divides the issue into four major sections. First, it considers the current statutory position concerning reports, including, where applicable, those relating to recommendations. We then consider early practice. More recent practice of the ombudsmen and associated case law is considered next. Finally, we draw our conclusions and make provisional proposals for reform.

## THE CURRENT STATUTORY POSITION

### Parliamentary Commissioner

#### Statement of reasons

6.3 If an investigation is not conducted, then a statement of reasons should, at the least, be sent to the Member of Parliament who forwarded the complaint to the Parliamentary Commissioner.[1] There are no relevant provisions directly mentioning the discontinuance of an opened investigation. However, as section 10 of the Parliamentary Commissioner Act 1967 refers to "conducted" rather than "completed" investigations then we suggest that a statement of reasons should also be sent to the relevant Member in this case.

#### Normal report

6.4 Section 10 of the Parliamentary Commissioner Act 1967 sets out the basic provisions for a report from the Parliamentary Commissioner. The first subsection of this requires the Parliamentary Commissioner to submit a report to the Member of Parliament who requested an investigation into maladministration under section 5(1) of the Act.

6.5 If an investigation is conducted, then the Parliamentary Commissioner shall also send a report to the principal officer of the relevant department or authority and anyone whose action is the subject of a complaint.[2]

6.6 This deals with ordinary cases. However, section 10(4) of the Parliamentary Commissioner Act 1967 allows the Parliamentary Commissioner to lay a report before each of the Houses of Parliament when they think fit. The practice has

---

[1] If the person who requested the investigation is no longer a Member of the House then the Parliamentary Commissioner should send the report to such Member as he or she thinks appropriate.

[2] Parliamentary Commissioner Act 1967, ss 10(2) and 10(2A).

developed that a report is laid when an investigation is of a general or highly political nature.

### Special report

6.7 Finally, if having issued a report, the Parliamentary Commissioner is of the opinion that "the injustice has not been, or will not be, remedied", then a "special Report" can be laid before Parliament. This may happen both for investigations into maladministration under section 5(1), and for breach of the "relevant duty" under section 5(1A).

### Effect

6.8 The Parliamentary Commissioner Act 1967 is silent as to the effects of any of these actions. As the Parliamentary Commissioner is an officer of the House of Commons, it seems that the process was designed to be worked out over time within Parliament. Below, we will consider how practice has developed and the effect of recent decisions of the courts.

6.9 To summarise, the options available to the Parliamentary Commissioner are:

(1) a statement of reasons, where an investigation is not conducted or is discontinued;

(2) a report, which may or may not be laid before each of the Houses of Parliament; or

(3) a special report, which shall be laid before each of the Houses of Parliament.

## Local Government Ombudsman

### Statement of reasons

6.10 If the Local Government Ombudsman decides not to investigate a complaint or decides to discontinue an investigation, then they should send those concerned a statement of reasons for so doing.[3] Additionally, if the ombudsman "is satisfied with action which the authority concerned have taken or propose to take" and decides "that it is not appropriate to prepare and send a copy of a report", then it merely has to send the people concerned a statement of reasons.[4]

### Normal report

6.11 The situation in relation to the Local Government Ombudsman is very different. There is no role for Parliament. Reports are governed by sections 30 and 31 of the Local Government Act 1974. The principal duty is that where the Local Government Ombudsman completes an investigation then they should send a

---

[3] Local Government Act 1974, s 30(1C).

[4] Local Government Act 1974, s 30(1B).

report to each of the persons concerned.[5] According to section 30(1D), a person concerned is defined as:

(1)    the complainant (if any);

(2)    the person who referred the matter (if any);[6]

(3)    the authority concerned; and

(4)    any other authority or person who is alleged in the complaint, or who otherwise appears to the Local Commissioner, to have taken or authorised the action which is or would be the subject of the investigation.

6.12    Under section 31 of the Local Government Act 1974, where the Local Government Ombudsman reports that there has been maladministration, "a failure in a service which it was the function of an authority to provide", or "a failure to provide such a service" then the authority should inform the ombudsman of the action it has taken or intends to take within three months.[7]

### Further report

6.13    If the Local Government Ombudsman does not receive a response from the authority, is not satisfied with the proposed action outlined by the authority, or does not receive confirmation that actions detailed have been undertaken, then the ombudsman shall issue a further report and make recommendations. When a further report is made then the authority should follow such actions detailed in the recommendations.[8]

6.14    This, however, is a relatively recent change to the statutory framework. As originally drafted, the Local Government Act 1974 was silent as to making recommendations and as to the effect of a second report. The first major change came with the Local Government Act 1988 which placed a duty on the authority to consider the second report.[9] More importantly, the Local Government and Housing Act 1989 made provisions for the second report to contain specific recommendations as to action that should be taken by the authority.[10]

---

[5]    Local Government Act 1974, s 30(1).

[6]    This is for a reference from a body listed in Local Government Act 1974, s 26C(2). This occurs where a complaint is made to an authority and it wishes to refer the matter to the LGO. This can only happen with the complainant's consent.

[7]    The 3 month time limit can be extended by the Local Government Ombudsman but only in writing: Local Government Act 1974, s 31(2).

[8]    Local Government Act 1974, s 31(2B).

[9]    Local Government Act 1974, s 31(2A) inserted by Local Government Act 1988, s 29 and sch 3, para 7.

[10]    The current version was inserted by the Local Government and Public Involvement in Health Act 2007, s 176(3) and reflects changes to the Local Government Ombudsman's overall jurisdiction – as set out in Part 2 of this consultation paper. The substantive relationship between the Local Government Ombudsman and the authority is identical, Local Government Act 1974, ss 31(2A), (2B) and (2BA).

*Effect*

6.15    The Act is silent as to the consequences of failing to implement the Local Government Ombudsman's recommendations, other than adverse publicity. Where the authority still fails to comply with the recommendations made by the Local Government Ombudsman, then the ombudsman can require the authority to publish a statement in two local publications. The statement includes the ombudsman's recommended action and any other material the ombudsman feels necessary.[11] However, it need only contain the authority's reasons for not having taken such action if the authority so requires.[12] This allows the authority to state its reasons for not complying with the ombudsman's recommendations but does not require it.

6.16    Consequently, the options available to the Local Government Ombudsman are in ascending order:

(1)    a statement of reasons, where an investigation is not opened or discontinued, or if a report is not issued following an investigation;

(2)    a normal report;

(3)    a further report, if not satisfied with the reaction to the normal report – this shall make recommendations; or

(4)    the publication of a statement in local press concerning the Local Government Ombudsman's investigation.

## Public Services Ombudsman for Wales

*Statement of reasons*

6.17    If the Public Services Ombudsman for Wales decides not to open an investigation, or to discontinue an existing investigation, then the ombudsman shall issue a statement of reasons for doing so to those concerned and any other person it thinks appropriate. He can, if it thinks fit, also publish the statement.[13]

*Standard process (sections 16 to 19 of the Public Services Ombudsman (Wales) Act 2005)*

6.18    After conducting an investigation, the Public Services Ombudsman for Wales must prepare a report and send this to the appropriate persons.[14] The appropriate persons are listed in section 16(2) of the Public Services Ombudsman (Wales) Act 2005, and include: "the person who made the complaint"; "the listed authority"; and "any other person who is alleged in the complaint to have taken or authorised the action complained of". The ombudsman can also send the report to any other person he sees as

---

[11]   Local Government Act 1974, ss 31(2D), (2E)(a), (2E)(b), and (2F).

[12]   Local Government Act 1974, s 31(2E)(c).

[13]   Public Services Ombudsman (Wales) Act 2005, s 12.

[14]   Public Services Ombudsman (Wales) Act 2005, s 16(1).

appropriate,[15] and publish the report generally, if he thinks it in the public interest to do so.[16]

6.19 If the authority receives a report then it should make the report available at one or more of its offices and publish it on its website, if it has one, for a period of three weeks.[17] The formal requirements can be dispensed with if the ombudsman so directs, but the ombudsman must take into account "the public interest", "the interests of the person aggrieved", and "the interests of any other persons he thinks appropriate".[18]

6.20 On receiving a report the authority must, within one month or such time as set in the report, notify the ombudsman of the action it proposes to take and the time period it proposes for taking such action.[19]

6.21 Collectively, sections 16 to 19 of the Public Services Ombudsman (Wales) Act 2005 form the normal process for issuing reports.

### Short-form process (section 21 of the Public Services Ombudsman (Wales) Act 2005)

6.22 Section 21 of the Public Services Ombudsman (Wales) Act 2005 provides for a more "light touch" reporting mechanism. This allows reports to be published without the provisions in sections 16 to 19 applying where the ombudsman is satisfied that the complainant has not suffered injustice or hardship[20] or – where the complainant has suffered injustice or hardship – the action taken or proposed by the authority is sufficient to meet his recommendations.[21] The ombudsman must also be satisfied that it is in the public interest to publish a report[22] but not in the public interest to use the standard process for this.[23]

### Special report

6.23 Section 22 of the Public Services Ombudsman (Wales) Act 2005 allows the ombudsman to issue a "special report" in the following cases relating to standard reports 19:

(1) where the ombudsman has not received notification form the authority under section 19, detailing the action the authority proposes to take;

---

[15] Public Services Ombudsman (Wales) Act 2005, s 16(3).

[16] Public Services Ombudsman (Wales) Act 2005, ss 16(4) and (5).

[17] Public Services Ombudsman (Wales) Act 2005, s 17(1). The authority has to state the period for which the three weeks will run and the offices at which the report will be available: Public Services Ombudsman (Wales) Act 2005, s 17(4).

[18] Public Services Ombudsman (Wales) Act 2005, s 16(8).

[19] Public Services Ombudsman (Wales) Act 2005, s 19.

[20] Public Services Ombudsman (Wales) Act 2005, s 21(1)(a).

[21] Public Services Ombudsman (Wales) Act 2005, ss 21(2)(a) and (b).

[22] Public Services Ombudsman (Wales) Act 2005, s 21(6).

[23] Public Services Ombudsman (Wales) Act 2005, s 21(1)(b) or s 21(2)(c).

(2) where he is not satisfied with the action taken or proposed by the authority; and

(3) where he does not think that the action to be undertaken by the authority will be completed within the permitted timescale set in the original report.[24]

6.24 A special report can also be issued where alternative action to address the complaint has been taken under section 3 of the Act or where a short-form report has been issued, and these approaches have not succeeded in achieving their aims.[25]

6.25 A special report must set out recommendations that should be undertaken to remedy any injustice or hardship and to prevent the same happening in the future.[26]

6.26 A special report is sent to the complainant, the authorities that are the subject of the complaint, all those who received the original sections 16 to 19 report and any other person that the ombudsman considers appropriate.[27] The report can be published. The cost of publication is met by the authority subject to the report rather than the ombudsman.[28] If the special report concerns the Welsh Assembly Government then it is laid before the National Assembly for Wales.[29]

6.27 Therefore, in relation to the Public Services Ombudsman for Wales, the following options are available:

(1) a statement of reasons, if the ombudsman does not open an investigation or discontinues an existing investigation;

(2) a standard report, under sections 16 to 19 of the Public Services Ombudsman (Wales) Act 2005;

(3) a short-form report, under section 21 of the Public Services Ombudsman (Wales) Act 2005; and

(4) a special report, which must contain recommendations to remedy any injustice or hardship and to prevent the same occurring again. This can be published and can, if concerning the Welsh Assembly Government, be laid before the National Assembly for Wales.

---

[24] Public Services Ombudsman (Wales) Act 2005, s 22(2).

[25] Public Services Ombudsman (Wales) Act 2005, ss 22(4) and (6).

[26] Public Services Ombudsman (Wales) Act 2005, s 22(8)(b).

[27] Public Services Ombudsman (Wales) Act 2005, ss 22(9)(b), 22(9)(a) and 22(10).

[28] Public Services Ombudsman (Wales) Act 2005, s 23.

[29] Public Services Ombudsman (Wales) Act 2005, s 24(2)(a).

**Health Service Ombudsman**

6.28    The reporting system for the Health Service Ombudsman is broadly similar to that for the Parliamentary Commissioner. Under section 14 of the Health Service Commissioners Act 1993, where an investigation is conducted, then a report should be sent to the complainant, the relevant health authority, any Members of Parliament who assisted in the making of the complaint, and the Secretary of State.[30] If an investigation is not conducted then a statement of reasons should be given to the complainant and any Member of Parliament who assisted in making the complaint.[31]

6.29    If, having made a report, the ombudsman thinks that any injustice or hardship sustained "has not been and will not be remedied" then the ombudsman can lay a "special report" before each of the Houses of Parliament if it so decides.[32] The ombudsman must lay an annual report before each of the Houses of Parliament and may lay such other reports as "he thinks fit".[33]

6.30    In relation to the Health Service Ombudsman the available options are:

(1)    a statement of reasons if not opening an investigation;

(2)    a report; and

(3)    a special report, which is laid before Parliament.

6.31    As with the Parliamentary Commissioner, the statute is silent as to the effect of these reports.

**Housing Ombudsman**

6.32    Determinations of the Housing Ombudsman are governed by paragraph 7 of schedule 2 to the Housing Act 1996. A determination may order a member of a scheme – which must include all social landlords – to pay compensation to complainants and order that the member, or the complainant, "shall not exercise or require the performance of any of the contractual or other obligations or rights existing between them".[34]

6.33    If the member fails to comply with a determination within a "reasonable time", the ombudsman "may order him to publish in such manner as the ombudsman sees fit that he has failed to comply with the determination".[35] If the member fails to do this then the ombudsman can publish and then recover the costs of such publication from the member.[36]

---

[30]    Health Service Commissioners Act 1993, ss 14(1), (2A), (2C) and (2E).

[31]    Health Service Commissioners Act 1993, ss 14(2), (2B), (2D) and (2F).

[32]    Health Service Commissioners Act 1993, s 14(3).

[33]    Health Service Commissioners Act 1993, s 14(4).

[34]    Housing Act 1996, sch 2, para 7(2).

[35]    Housing Act 1996, sch 2, para 7(3).

[36]    Housing Act 1996, sch 2, para 7(5).

6.34   Therefore, the options available to the Housing Ombudsman are:

(1)   issuing a determination of the matter; and

(2)   publication.

**EARLY PRACTICE**

6.35   This section considers the practice and early case law on the Parliamentary Commissioner and the Local Government Ombudsman. We focus on these ombudsmen as the provisions of the Health Service Ombudsman are broadly similar to those of the Parliamentary Commissioner. The Public Services Ombudsman for Wales is a more recent addition to the public services ombudsmen family, so is considered below. The Housing Ombudsman is also excluded as it is both more recent and its determinations have not attracted the same level of political debate as those of the Parliamentary Commissioner.

6.36   In relation to the Parliamentary Commissioner, the wide drafting of the Act meant that practice had to develop in relation to the effects of a report and how to resolve disputes between the Parliamentary Commissioner and the Government. The vast majority of the Parliamentary Commissioner's reports have been accepted. However, there have been some notable exceptions to this.

6.37   The first Parliamentary Commissioner made early use of the provisions in section 10(4) of the Parliamentary Commissioner Act 1967. This was in the third report of his first session, in relation to complaints made against the Foreign Office concerning the non-payment of compensation for certain detainees at Sachsenhausen during the Second World War.[37] This investigation essentially turned on the finding by the Foreign Office that the camps the complainants had been detained in were satellites to the main concentration camp and therefore that their detention – though harsh – did not bear the hallmark nature of a concentration camp. On this basis the complainants were ineligible for compensation under the Anglo-German Agreement of 1964, as administered by the Foreign Office. In making a finding of maladministration, the Parliamentary Commissioner concluded that the process was flawed as it relied on "partial and largely irrelevant information".[38] It was "biased against the complainants".[39] He recommended that the Foreign Office review the evidence and take a fresh decision in each case.[40] Though payments were eventually made, the Government did not accept the findings of maladministration.

6.38   The potential weaknesses in the Parliamentary Commissioner's reporting system can be seen in relation to *Court Line*.[41] This concerned the failure of a holiday company on 15 August 1974. The then Parliamentary Commissioner, Alan Marre,

---

[37]   Third Report of the Parliamentary Commissioner for Administration (1967-68) HC 54 (*Sachsenhausen*).

[38]   *Sachsenhausen*, para 63(1).

[39]   *Sachsenhausen*, para 57.

[40]   *Sachsenhausen*, para 70.

[41]   Fifth Report of the Parliamentary Commissioner for Administration (1974-75) HC 498 (*Court Line*).

also decided to use the provisions of section 10(4) of the Parliamentary Commissioner Act 1967 and lay his report before Parliament.

6.39 In reaching a finding of maladministration, the Parliamentary Commissioner expressed himself thus:

> The test I have sought to apply is whether, on an objective consideration and disregarding the subsequent course of events, the statements were fully appropriate as known at the time ...

> ... there was [a] need to give persons who were deciding whether to spend their own money on holiday arrangements a balanced enough assessment on which to base their decisions.[42]

6.40 Whilst the Parliamentary Commissioner was preparing his report, the Government introduced a bill to set up a financial scheme that would cover those adversely affected by the collapse of holiday companies, which became the Air Travel Reserve Fund Act 1975. As the Act had retrospective effect back one year, those affected by the collapse of Court Line could make claims against that fund.

6.41 The Government disagreed with the findings of maladministration made by the Parliamentary Commissioner in his report. This led, eventually, to a vote on the report by the House of Commons. This split along party lines, and therefore the Government won.[43] One particularly interesting aspect in the *Court Line* investigation was the extent to which the Parliamentary Commissioner was prepared to engage with a factual analysis of the options open to the Secretary of State, and take a judgment as to the proper approach to the facts before him.

6.42 The factual background to *Court Line* was complicated and there were many thousands potentially affected by the Government's actions. However, the next major investigation by the Parliamentary Commissioner, that into *Barlow Clowes*, was of an altogether different scale and ran from 1988 to 1990.[44] There were complaints referred by 159 MPs,[45] the report came to 170 pages and concerned the collapse of a financial services group. This was by far the largest investigation yet mounted by the Parliamentary Commissioner. The effect of the Parliamentary Commissioner's findings and the response of Government is particularly illuminating. This is especially the case when considering the position that we have reached today with the current Parliamentary Commissioner's multiple reports on occupational pensions and Equitable Life.

6.43 As with earlier examples, *Barlow Clowes* was laid before Parliament under section 10(4) of the Parliamentary Commissioner Act 1967. In relation to the prudential regulation of Barlow Clowes, the Parliamentary Commissioner made a

---

[42] *Court Line*, para 91.

[43] *Hansard* (HC), 6 August 1975, vol 897, col 586.

[44] First Report Session of the Parliamentary Commissioner for Administration (1989-90) HC 76 (*Barlow Clowes*).

[45] R Gregory and G Drewry, "Barlow Clowes and the Ombudsman: Part 1" [1991] *Public Law* 192.

series of telling findings of maladministration.[46] On the basis of this, he recommended the payment of compensation to those adversely affected by the group's collapse.[47]

6.44 Discussions with the Government on the work of the Parliamentary Commissioner were conducted – as envisaged within the statute – whilst the Parliamentary Commissioner was preparing his report. It emerged within these discussions that the Government disagreed with both the findings relating to maladministration and the compensatory recommendation.[48] The Government stated that it was going to propose a different scheme. An overview of these discussions is included at the end of the Parliamentary Commissioner's report. Although the Parliamentary Commissioner felt that his proposals were preferable, he concluded his report by stating that he: "could not say, in all the circumstances, that the Government's proposals would not constitute a fair remedy for the injustice which had been suffered".[49]

6.45 In response to the Parliamentary Commissioner's report, the Government issued a detailed response as to how it viewed the role of regulation and the particular findings of the Parliamentary Commissioner.[50] The Government rejected the findings of maladministration. It asserted that, at all times, the action of the department was "careful and considered and its actions reasonable".[51] It also asserted that it had "no legal liability to pay compensation".[52] On the latter point, it was, of course, correct. However, it went on to recognise a "number of unusual features which distinguish it from other business failures".[53] This included the very large number of investors in Barlow Clowes.[54] Consequently the Government felt able, in such "exceptional circumstances", "to offer a substantial payment, without admission of fault or liability, to investors in Barlow Clowes".[55]

6.46 The Government took steps to address the issues raised by the Parliamentary Commissioner. However, in each of these cases, the steps taken were in the context of a rejection of the findings and recommendations of the Parliamentary Commissioner and the inability of Parliament to force Government into accepting a finding of maladministration.

6.47 In relation to the Local Government Ombudsman, the picture is revealing. In its early history there was a problem with local authorities failing to implement the

---

[46] *Barlow Clowes*, paras 8.1 to 8.13.

[47] *Barlow Clowes*, paras 8.14 to 8.16.

[48] *Barlow Clowes*, paras 8.17 to 8.20.

[49] *Barlow Clowes*, para 8.21.

[50] Observations by the Government on the Report of the Parliamentary Commissioner for Administration on Barlow Clowes (1989-90) HC 99 (*Government observations on Barlow Clowes*).

[51] *Government observations on Barlow Clowes*, para 37.

[52] *Government observations on Barlow Clowes*, para 37.

[53] *Government observations on Barlow Clowes*, para 38.

[54] *Government observations on Barlow Clowes*, para 39.

[55] *Government observations on Barlow Clowes*, para 43.

reports of the Local Government Ombudsman. Nearly 10% of Local Government Ombudsman reports were at one stage being rejected by local authorities.[56]

6.48   However, recently that position has changed, with rejection only taking place in 0.6% of cases.[57] The implementation of the Local Government Ombudsman's reports went up dramatically after the courts clarified the underlying relationship between a local authority and a report issued by the Local Government Ombudsman.

6.49   In *R v Local Commissioner, ex parte Eastleigh Borough Council*, a local authority challenged the Local Government Ombudsman's findings on various grounds. The Court of Appeal decided against Eastleigh. Lord Donaldson of Lymington MR set out what he considered to be the correct view of the relationship between the local authority and the ombudsman:

> There is the suggestion that the council should issue a statement disputing the right of the ombudsman to make his findings and that this would provide the council with an adequate remedy. Such an action would wholly undermine the system of ombudsman's reports and would, in effect, provide for an appeal to the media against his findings. The parliamentary intention was that reports by ombudsmen should be loyally accepted by the local authorities concerned. This is clear from section 30(4) and (5), which require the local authority to make the report available for inspection by the public and to advertise this fact, from section 31(1), which requires the local authority to notify the ombudsman of the action which it has taken and proposes to take in the light of his report and from section 31(2), which entitles the ombudsman to make a further report if the local authority's response is not satisfactory.[58]

6.50   It follows that the only way to dispute the findings of the Local Government Ombudsman is to challenge the report itself.

---

[56]   www.lgo.org.uk. On average some 6% have not been implemented: M Seneviratne, *Ombudsmen: Public services and administrative justice* (2002) p 218.

[57]   www.lgo.org.uk.

[58]   *R v Local Commissioner for Administration for the South, the West Midlands, Leicestershire, Lincolnshire and Cambridgeshire, ex parte Eastleigh Borough Council* [1988] QB 855. The legislation has been amended subsequently. However, the differences are immaterial for present purposes and the statement from Lord Donaldson was reaffirmed recently by Wall LJ in the Court of Appeal: *R (Bradley) v Secretary of State for Work and Pensions* [2008] EWCA Civ 36, [2009] QB 114 at [139].

## RECENT PRACTICE AND ASSOCIATED CASE LAW

6.51 The position of the findings and recommendations made by the Parliamentary Commissioner and the Local Government Ombudsman has recently been re-examined by the courts in two cases, *Bradley* and *Equitable Members Action Group*.[59] The leading authority is that of *Bradley* in the Court of Appeal.

6.52 *Bradley* arose from the Parliamentary Commissioner's special report on *Occupational Pensions*.[60] This concerned several thousand private sector employees who lost their final salary pensions when their pension schemes were wound up. The Parliamentary Commissioner opened a large scale investigation into a failure of prudential regulation by the Department of Work and Pensions.

6.53 Government rejected the ombudsman's initial findings of maladministration. In support of the Parliamentary Commissioner, the Public Administration Select Committee produced its own report.[61]

6.54 The Parliamentary Commissioner had made five recommendations, the crucial one being the first:

> I recommend that the Government should consider whether it should make arrangements for the restoration of the core pension and non-core benefits promised to all those whom I have identified above are fully covered by my recommendations – by whichever means is most appropriate, including if necessary by payment from public funds, to replace the full amount lost by those individuals.[62]

6.55 Before the Administrative Court, counsel for the claimants conceded that the Parliamentary Commissioner's recommendations could not be binding on the Secretary of State, but argued that findings were. Mr Justice Bean held that the Secretary of State was bound by the Parliamentary Commissioner's first finding of maladministration, that the Government had issued misleading official information. He held that it was irrational for the Secretary of State to reject the Parliamentary Commissioner's findings.[63] Accordingly, the court quashed the Department of Work and Pensions' decision to reject that finding, and directed that the decision to reject the first recommendation restoring benefits be reconsidered.

6.56 On this particular issue the Court of Appeal decided that the Minister could reject the Parliamentary Commissioner's findings where he had "cogent reasons" to do

---

[59] *R (Equitable Members Action Group) v HM Treasury* [2009] EWHC 2495 (Admin), (2009) 159 NLJ 1514; *R (Bradley) v Secretary of State for Work and Pensions* [2008] EWCA Civ 36, [2009] QB 114.

[60] Trusting in the pensions promise: government bodies and the security of final salary occupational pensions, Report of the Parliamentary and Health Service Ombudsman (2005-06) HC 984 (*Occupational Pensions*).

[61] The Ombudsman in Question: the ombudsman's report on pensions and its constitutional implications, Report of the Public Administration Select Committee (2006-07) HC 1081.

[62] *Occupational Pensions*, para 615.

[63] *R (Bradley) v Secretary of State for Work and Pensions* [2007] EWHC 242 (Admin) [2007] Pens LR 87 at [85].

so. Specifically, the Court endorsed the following sentence in the skeleton argument:

> The question is not whether the defendant himself considers that there was maladministration, but whether in the circumstances his rejection of the ombudsman's finding to this effect is based on cogent reasons.[64]

6.57    The court based this view on the scheme of the Parliamentary Commissioner Act 1967, and distinguished the position of the Parliamentary Commissioner from the Local Government Ombudsman. It thereby took a substantially different position to that taken by Mr Justice Bean in the Administrative Court. In particular the court noted that:

> The purpose for which the legislation was introduced was to give Members of Parliament – in particular, Members of the House of Commons – access to the services of an independent and authoritative investigator as "a better instrument which they can use to protect the citizen".[65]

6.58    The Court of Appeal did not accept that there was a pure choice; it was not a question of the Secretary of State's preference. Nor was there any question that the findings of the Parliamentary Commissioner should be binding – Parliament had the opportunity to make that the case and chose not to.

6.59    The courts' involvement was only one episode in a broader political controversy. The Government rejected the findings of maladministration and the recommendations of the Parliamentary Commissioner. Nevertheless, substantial relief was in the end made available to a large proportion of affected individuals. About the same time as the judicial review proceedings were going on, the Financial Assistance Scheme was created on the initiative of the Department of Work and Pensions. In December 2006, the scheme was extended to cover those within 15 years of their scheme's pension age. Subsequently, the scheme was expanded further still, so as to ensure that all members of affected schemes would receive 80% of their core pension entitlements.[66] The relevant statutory provisions are contained in Part 2 of the Pensions Act 2007.

6.60    Examining the recent case law, Kirkham and others suggest that *Bradley* was correct to leave the political process as the primary place for the discussion of ombudsmen's reports.[67] Our conclusions on this are discussed in the next section.

---

[64]    *R (Bradley) v Secretary of State for Work and Pensions* [2008] EWCA Civ 36, [2009] QB 114 at [72] by Sir John Chadwick.

[65]    Above, at [40] by Sir John Chadwick.

[66]    The Pensions Bill: Government Undertakings relating to the Financial Assistance Scheme, Report of the Public Administration Select Committee (2006-07) HC 523.

[67]    R Kirkham, B Thompson and T Buck, "When putting things right goes wrong: enforcing the recommendations of the ombudsman" [2008] *Public Law* 510.

6.61 Finally, in relation to the Local Government Ombudsman, the Court of Appeal in *Bradley* referred to *ex parte Eastleigh Borough Council*. Lord Justice Wall concluded that:

> It is true that the citizen could apply for judicial review of the local authority's decision not to implement the [Local Government Ombudsman's] findings, but the system, as I understand it, depends upon the convention that local authorities will be bound by the findings of the [Local Government Ombudsman]. It must follow inexorably that if a local authority wishes to avoid findings of maladministration made by a [Local Government Ombudsman], it must apply for judicial review to quash the decision.[68]

6.62 Therefore one of the many interesting outcomes of *Bradley* is that the Court of Appeal leant its weight to the statements of Lord Donaldson MR in *ex parte Eastleigh*. As Kirkham and others put it:

> The most curious feature of the ruling in *Bradley*, however, is that it appears to have confirmed in law a position that no one asked for and few people were aware of – that the findings of the [Local Government Ombudsman] are binding, provided they are made within the law.[69]

6.63 This issue was returned to in *Equitable Life*. This is by far the largest investigation ever undertaken by the Parliamentary Commissioner and concerned severe failure in the prudential regulation of a large mutual insurance institution.[70] The Parliamentary Commissioner's first report was endorsed by the Public Administration Select Committee. This was rejected by Government. The rejection of the Parliamentary Commissioner's findings led the Public Administration Select Committee to issue a further report. This was followed by a special report from the Parliamentary Commissioner. Both of these were also rejected by Government, leading to two special reports from the Public Administration Select Committee.[71]

---

[68] *R (Bradley) v Secretary of State for Work and Pensions* [2008] EWCA Civ 36, [2009] QB 114 at [139], by Wall LJ.

[69] R Kirkham, B Thompson and T Buck, "When putting things right goes wrong: enforcing the recommendations of the ombudsman" [2008] *Public Law* 510, 530.

[70] Equitable Life: a decade of regulatory failure, Report of the Parliamentary and Health Service Ombudsman (2007-08) HC 815.

[71] Justice delayed: The Ombudsman's report on Equitable Life, Report of the Public Administration Select Committee (2008-09) HC 41. Justice denied? The Government's response to the Ombudsman's report on Equitable Life, Report of the Public Administration Select Committee (2008-09) HC 219. Justice denied? Government Response to the Committee's Sixth Report of Session 2008-09, Special Report of the Public Administration Select Committee (2008-09) HC 569. Justice delayed: The Ombudsman's report on Equitable Life: Government Response to the Committee's Second Report of Session 2008-09, Special Report of the Public Administration Select Committee (2008-09) HC 953. The special reports were issued to the House under Standing Order 133.

6.64    The Administrative Court then reaffirmed the position in *Bradley* that the Parliamentary Commissioner had to be viewed in the context of its relationship with Parliament. Consequently, the Court held that the primary place for the enforcement of an ombudsman's findings was Parliament.[72]

6.65    Though, as we set out above, there was considerable support given to the Parliamentary Commissioner by the Public Administration Select Committee, the then Government rejected both the findings and recommendations made by the Parliamentary Commissioner. The change in attitude to the situation only came with a change in Government following the election of 2010. The Coalition Agreement of 2010 states that the Government will "implement the Parliamentary and Health Service Ombudsman's recommendation to make fair and transparent payments to Equitable Life policy holders".[73]

6.66    In relation to special reports from the Local Government Ombudsman, a recent notable example is *Memorial safety*.[74] This was the first such report made jointly with the Public Services Ombudsman for Wales. *Memorial safety* addressed a recurring problem that the Local Government Ombudsman and the Public Services Ombudsman for Wales had identified in complaints made to them. The matter – that of local authorities laying down headstones due to a perceived health and safety risk of them injuring cemetery users – had also been the subject of a campaign in the national press. There are two significant aspects to this report. It demonstrates the public services ombudsmen's response to a press campaign and it is also the first joint report between the Public Services Ombudsman for Wales and the Local Government Ombudsman.

### General reports and other documents

6.67    Reviews of local authorities' performance are published annually. These are of a different nature to the special reports of the Local Government Ombudsman. They highlight the performance of authorities across various areas and draw out particular issues of importance in that year.[75] Such reports allow for a comparative approach to the performance of different local authorities.

6.68    Finally, there are those publications which are focused either purely or principally on general governance issues. These build on the experience of the ombudsmen in handling complaints but their focus is on preventing future service failure rather than remedying injustice. The methodology here differs between the ombudsmen. The special report of the Local Government Ombudsman *Local partnerships* focused on improving administrative practice in an area where it was suggested that the lines of accountability could be difficult to ascertain.[76] In demonstrating the problem it used specific case examples. A similar approach

---

[72]    *R (Equitable Members Action Group) v HM Treasury* [2009] EWHC 2495 (Admin), (2009) 159 NLJ 1514.

[73]    HM Government, *The Coalition: our programme for government* (2010) p 26.

[74]    Local Government Ombudsman and Public Services Ombudsman for Wales, *Special Report, Memorial safety in local authority cemeteries* (2006) (*Memorial safety*).

[75]    http://www.lgo.org.uk/CouncilsPerformance (last visited 16 August 2010).

[76]    Local Government Ombudsman, *Special Report, Local partnerships and citizen redress* (2007) (*Local partnerships*).

was adopted by the Parliamentary Commissioner in the report *Improving public services*.[77]

6.69 These contrast with the Parliamentary Commissioner's *Principles of good administration*,[78] which sets out pure principles. The principles were widely distributed to governmental bodies and are now also annexed to *Managing public money*, which is the core document for central government expenditure.[79]

6.70 The value of pure principles and the continuing need for specific examples can be seen in the publications of both ombudsmen. *Improving public services* relied on the recently published *Principles of good administration* when working through examples. *Local partnerships* used examples within the single document to highlight problems that the general approach was seeking to address.

## CONCLUSIONS AND PROVISIONAL PROPOSALS

6.71 In approaching this, we split our conclusions and provisional proposals into three subheadings: provisions for issuing reports on investigations; the status of findings and recommendations; and more general reporting provisions.

### Reports resulting from individual investigations

6.72 Here we consider the types of reports that could be available to the public services ombudsmen resulting from an investigation into potential maladministration on the part of a public body. This includes questions as to the findings and recommendations of such reports.

### *Types of report*

6.73 It is clear that the approach contained in the Parliamentary Commissioner Act 1967 is very different from that in the Public Services Ombudsman (Wales) Act 2005. On the one hand, this can be attributed to the relationship the Parliamentary Commissioner enjoys with Parliament. On the other, it also reflects developments in the governing thinking on ombudsmen – for instance, possible advantages of a "light touch" mechanism for issuing reports.

6.74 In relation to issuing different types of report, all the statutory regimes allow for this except that for the Housing Ombudsman. The most developed, we think, is that for the Public Services Ombudsman for Wales.

6.75 It is important to have a clear set of rules relating to the form of report issued, or a statement explaining the ombudsman's reasoning if the ombudsman is not opening an investigation. The decisions and reasoning of the public services ombudsmen should be available in an easily accessible manner to those affected by a complaint, interested in the workings of public bodies, or watching the ombudsmen.

---

[77] Improving public services: a matter of principle, Report of the Parliamentary and Health Service Ombudsman (2008-09) HC 9 (*Improving public services*).

[78] Parliamentary and Health Service Ombudsman, *Principles of good administration* (2007).

[79] HM Treasury, *Managing public money* (2007).

6.76    We conclude that there should be a common system for issuing reports and disseminating decisions. These should show the reasoning behind the decisions taken by the ombudsmen. We make provisional proposals on the matter below.

6.77    We consider that the model adopted for the Public Services Ombudsman for Wales should be adopted, with a slight variation, concerning the three types of report. However, we think that the difference between the various types of report should be made clearer to complainants, authorities and independent observers.

6.78    Therefore we suggest that in order to delineate the differences clearly to the public, the equivalent approach to that currently in section 21 of the Public Services Ombudsman (Wales) Act 2005 should be known as a "short-form report". We also provisionally propose that section 21 should be amended accordingly.

6.79    Therefore, for the Local Government Ombudsman there would be three types of report. The least intrusive approach would just have a simple "short-form report". The middle type would be the normal approach, and would also be known as a "report". The last type would be reserved for failure to implement original report, and would be known as "special reports".

6.80    The same approach should be adopted for the Parliamentary Commissioner, with three types of report being available. However, the ability to lay reports before each of the Houses of Parliament, currently contained in section 10(4) of the Parliamentary Commissioner Act 1967, should be retained in relation to both "reports" and "special reports".

6.81    We think that the approach adopted for the Health Service Ombudsman should be the same as that for the Parliamentary Commissioner.

6.82    **Do consultees agree that adopting a graduated approach to three different types of report, based on that already in place for the Public Services Ombudsman for Wales, would be desirable for each of the public services ombudsmen except the Housing Ombudsman?**

6.83    **Do consultees agree that these should be known as "short-form report", "report" and "special report"?**

6.84    **We provisionally propose that in order to ensure greater transparency, where the public ombudsmen decline to commence an investigation, or decide to abandon an existing investigation, there should be a statutory requirement to publish a "statement of reasons", setting out clearly the reasons for their decision.**

6.85    We think the nature of the Housing Ombudsman means that the basic approach in the current regime should continue. However, **we provisionally propose that the Housing Ombudsman's determinations should be recast as reports where they relate to social housing.** This would be the only type of report that the Housing Ombudsman would issue.

6.86    Finally, there is an issue that flows from our discussion in Part 5 on the need for greater transparency in the ombudsman process. This is whether the general principle that ombudsmen reports are anonymous as to the complainant and other individuals involved can be departed from. We do not have strong views on the matter. For some complainants it may be that they would wish to have their name associated with the report in order to vindicate their assertion that maladministration and injustice had affected them. However, there may be other reasons for not identifying the complainant or other individuals – as it could put others at risk. **We provisionally propose that ombudsmen should routinely ask complainants whether they want to be anonymous.** Lastly, **we provisionally propose that the ombudsmen should not be able to identify a complainant or other individual without their consent.**

### Findings and recommendations

6.87 In *Bradley* and *Equitable Members Action Group*, as in academic literature, a distinction was drawn between the findings and the recommendations of an ombudsman. Findings, here, includes those of fact and whether maladministration or injustice had occurred. Recommendations are the steps suggested to remedy the injustice and, where this is felt necessary, to prevent the same occurring in the future.

6.88 We think that the distinction between findings and recommendations is a useful one, as it sets out simply the issues for those reading the reports. The distinction is obvious enough in general legal terms and the term "recommendation" already exists in the relevant statute law. Therefore, we provisionally propose that subsequent amendments to the statutes use these terms.

6.89 **Do consultees agree that the governing statutes should draw a distinction between findings and recommendations and use those terms?**

6.90 "Recommendations" as a term is already used in the governing statutes for the public services ombudsmen. Therefore we do not think it needs a statutory definition. However, findings would be a new concept for the governing statutes. Therefore, **we provisionally propose that there should be a statutory definition for findings. This should include findings of fact and whether there was maladministration and injustice.**

### Status of findings and recommendations

6.91 The statutory regimes which underpin the actions of the ombudsmen are similar in one particular way. They rely on publicity, whether in Parliament, the National Assembly for Wales or local press, as the primary mechanism with which to encourage the implementation of reports. Within the bare statutory schemes, the final weapon available to any of the ombudsmen is not a binding order or a declaration that the public authority had acted in an illegal manner. Rather, it is the placement of their findings and recommendations in the public sphere. In some cases, the statute requires the authority to publish this. In others, there is a power to place a report before an elected body – either the Houses of Parliament or the National Assembly of Wales.

6.92 The current state of case law in *Bradley* and *Equitable Members Action Group* follows this basic principle and effectively leaves courts outside any debate on the merits of recommendations of the Parliamentary Commissioner. In relation to findings, the Government should only reject the Parliamentary Commissioner's findings when it gives "cogent reasons" for doing so.

6.93    The position, following *ex parte Eastleigh* and *Bradley*, in relation to the Local Government Ombudsman is very different. Here the findings of the Local Government Ombudsman are effectively binding unless successfully challenged by way of judicial review.

6.94    The implementation of any recommendation would almost always have an effect on the distribution of public resources. The proper place for such discussions is not in a court or similar body, which would be the ultimate effect of giving them a binding quality. To make recommendations binding would change the nature of the relationship between ombudsmen and those they oversee, removing the proper discussion and the collaborative approach that the original drafters saw as part of the ombudsman process – as we set out in Part 2.

6.95    Therefore, in relation to recommendations, we think that the approach adopted by the courts in relation to the Parliamentary Commissioner is broadly correct. **We provisionally conclude that the proper approach to recommendations is as part of the political process.**

6.96    Concerning findings, however, we think that the position is slightly different. The finding of maladministration should be, primarily, the role of ombudsmen and a judgment that Parliament has entrusted to them through their governing statutes. Obviously, whatever the position, a decision which is illegal in administrative law terms would be susceptible to judicial review. However, this is different from the current situation. The mere necessity to find "cogent reasons" before being able to reject the findings of the ombudsmen does not really protect the core competence of the Parliamentary Commissioner.

6.97    We suggest that *Bradley* and *Equitable Members Action Group* did not go far enough in respect of this matter. The argument in both *Bradley* and *Equitable Members Action Group* was that this would be placed better in terms of the relationship that the Parliamentary Commissioner has with Parliament. However, past practice shows that it is in fact quite likely that the Government will be able to reject the Parliamentary Commissioner's finding of maladministration and that Parliament will be unable to force the Government, which through its majority effectively controls the House of Commons, to accept the ombudsman's view.

6.98    In all of the examples given above, where the findings were not accepted the involvement of the Select Committee (now the Public Administration Select Committee), though supportive, did not change the position of the Government. *Court Line* gives probably the starkest example of how the relationship plays out, as this led to a vote in the House of Commons. The Commons divided on party lines and the then Government won.

6.99    The effect of the current relationship is that the Government can be the judge in its own cause, which – it seems to us – goes against the allocation of competences inherent in the Parliamentary Commissioner Act 1967.

6.100   We accept that in the cases considered in this Part, the Government went on to take some form of remedial action, as happened with *Sachsenhausen*, *Court Line* and *Barlow Clowes*, as well as the most recent cases – *Occupational Pensions* and *Equitable Life*. In the case of the latter, the Coalition Agreement of 2010 states that the Government will pay compensation.[80]

6.101  In the next Part we detail how recent developments within the House of Commons may have strengthened the position of the Select Committee – if the Select Committee supports the ombudsman. However, these developments do not change our initial view that a finding of maladministration is primarily the province of the relevant ombudsman, including the Parliamentary Commissioner, and that this should be protected.

6.102  Consequently, our provisional conclusion is that the current case law does not go far enough to protect the findings of the Parliamentary Commissioner.

6.103  We prefer the position in *ex parte Eastleigh*, which essentially protects the preserve of the ombudsman unless illegality in an administrative law sense can be shown – which would include coming to a conclusion that no rational ombudsman could come to.

6.104  Commenting on the effect that *Bradley* may have on the other ombudsmen, Kirkham and others thought it likely that the courts would follow the same line for the Health Service Ombudsman and the Public Services Ombudsman for Wales. This was on the basis of their having a relationship with an elected body.[81]

6.105  In respect of the Housing Ombudsman, its relationship with members of an approved scheme is very different to those that the other ombudsmen have with the bodies within their jurisdiction. There is also no formal relationship between the Housing Ombudsman and an elected body. It is, therefore, impossible to predict what would develop in the future as to the status of its determinations.

6.106  We think that this could lead, potentially, to courts adopting a position on findings that we do not favour. Therefore, we suggest that the situation in relation to these public services ombudsmen should also be clarified in statutory provisions.

6.107  **We provisionally propose that a public body should only be able to reject the findings in a report of a public services ombudsman following the successful judicial review of that report.**

### Issuing general reports

6.108  The above concerns reports relating to individual or systemic failure. Ombudsmen, as we noted above and in Part 2, have a wider role than this. We think that all of the ombudsmen should have a specific power to publish principles of good administration and codes of practice. This would build on their work as complaints handlers but is not pinned to individual failures or complaints.

6.109  There is a specific power to issues guidance on "good administrative practice" in section 31(1) of the Public Services Ombudsman (Wales) Act 2005, although

---

[80]  HM Government, *The Coalition: our programme for Government* (2010) p 26.

[81]  R Kirkham, B Thompson and T Buck, "When putting things right goes wrong: enforcing the recommendations of the ombudsman" [2008] *Public Law* 510.

there is no equivalent in the governing statutes of the other public services ombudsmen.

6.110   There are also provisions whereby both the Parliamentary Commissioner and the Health Service Ombudsman can lay before Parliament such reports into their activity as they think fit.[82]

6.111   We think that the recent development of publishing principles and showing broad examples of best practice is to be encouraged. Ombudsmen are in a unique position as an independent redress mechanism with the capacity to produce such material. This is something that a court could not do, nor could individual tribunals. We also think that publishing data that allows for the comparative analysis of the performance of those subject to the public services ombudsmen's jurisdiction is extremely useful and fits with the audit approach adopted in the Coalition Agreement of 2010. Such an approach allows for the better functioning of governance networks, the encouragement of which, we suggest, is an important task for the public services ombudsmen.

6.112   A risk here is that there is overlap with the role of other bodies, such as the Administrative Justice and Tribunals Council.[83] However, we do not think this is necessarily problematic, as there are close links between the public services ombudsmen and such bodies – so potential duplication should be avoided. In fact, we are of the opinion that, where there is overlap between such institutions and organisations, this provides an opportunity for sharing best practice amongst those involved in administrative redress.

6.113   It is anomalous that some public services ombudsmen's statutes confer a specific power to publish such documents, while others do not. It may be that a specific statutory provision is strictly unnecessary – publication might properly be seen as incidental to the ombudsmen's core statutory responsibilities. Nevertheless, we think it would be clearer and more satisfactory if all the statutes had similar provisions.

6.114   We do not, however, feel that it would be appropriate to give such principles or codes of practice legal effect. The purpose of these would be to suggest good practice based on the ombudsmen's knowledge of the public sector rather than to allow additional regulatory burdens to be imposed on the public sector.

6.115   **Do consultees agree that there should be a specific statutory power for each of the public services ombudsmen to publish guidance, principles of good administration and codes of practice?**

---

[82]   Parliamentary Commissioner Act 1967, s 10(4) and Health Service Commissioners Act 1993, s 14(4)(b).

[83]   The Administrative Justice and Tribunals Council recently consulted on potential principles of administrative justice: *Principles of administrative justice – consultation draft* (2010).

# PART 7
# RELATIONSHIP WITH ELECTED BODIES

## INTRODUCTION

7.1 As we stated in Part 6, publicity is key to the ability of the public services ombudsmen to secure the implementation of their reports – especially given the non-binding nature of their recommendations. Elected bodies provide an excellent forum for the discussion of issues raised in reports and involvement in the political arena is of a distinct advantage to ombudsmen in pursuing the functions ascribed to them by statute.

7.2 In this part we discuss this matter in greater detail. We set out the powers available to the public services ombudsmen to lay reports before an appropriate elected body. We outline recent changes in Parliament that may assist the public services ombudsmen in their work. Finally we draw some conclusions and make certain provisional proposals that we hope would aid the work of all the ombudsmen through greater involvement with public bodies.

## CURRENT POSITION

7.3 Here we draw on three different reporting mechanisms that may be of use to the ombudsmen and show what powers exist, or not, for each of the public services ombudsmen. In doing this, we break the section down on the basis of: reports on individual investigations, annual reports, and general reports and other documents.

### Reports on individual investigations

7.4 Here we are considering both those reports which result from individual complaints and others which ombudsmen issue regarding systemic concerns that may have developed initially from individual complaints.

7.5 As noted in Part 6, the Parliamentary Commissioner can lay reports before both Houses of Parliament, as can the Health Service Ombudsman. As we explained in Part 6, the relationship with Parliament, and particularly with the Public Administration Select Committee that examines special reports laid before the House, is of exceptional value to the Parliamentary Commissioner.

7.6 The Public Services Ombudsman for Wales can lay its special reports before the National Assembly for Wales.

7.7 There is no relationship with elected bodies on reports that result from individual investigations for the Local Government Ombudsman or the Housing Ombudsman.

### Annual reports

7.8 Annual reports play a part in highlighting the breadth of work undertaken by an institution. They also highlight recurring problems and allow for the oversight of the ombudsmen by an elected body.

7.9　The increased role of select committees in the selection of public services ombudsmen has been a non-statutory development. However, all the statutes governing the public services ombudsmen make provision for reports to be made to their respective elected bodies. Of these statutory relationships, the two that have been developed most fully are those of the Parliamentary Commissioner and Health Service Ombudsman.

7.10　Under section 10(4) of the Parliamentary Commissioner Act 1967, the "Commissioner shall annually lay before each House of Parliament a general report on the performance of his functions under this Act". Similar provision is made by section 14(4) of the Health Service Commissioners Act 1993. In order to facilitate the work of the Parliamentary Commissioner, Standing Order 146 of the House of Commons tasks the Public Administration Select Committee with examining the reports of the Parliamentary Commissioner and the Health Service Ombudsman laid before the House. This includes both annual reports and special reports on individual investigations.

7.11　The Public Services Ombudsman for Wales must prepare an annual report on the discharge of his functions. This must be laid before the National Assembly for Wales and sent to the Welsh Assembly Government.[1]

7.12　Under Standing Order 7.61 of the National Assembly for Wales, time must be made available each year to debate the annual report of the Public Services Ombudsman for Wales. The Audit Committee should also consider the submitted accounts of the Ombudsman.[2] The practice has developed whereby the ombudsman appears before them.

7.13　The Local Government Ombudsman must lay its annual report before Parliament.[3] This is a recent alteration to the governing statute, following the Local Government and Public Involvement in Health Act 2007.[4] Before then, there was no direct relationship with Parliament.

7.14　The Housing Ombudsman sends its annual report to the Secretary of State and the board of Independent Housing Ombudsman Limited.[5] There is no direct relationship with Parliament.

**General reports or other documents**

7.15　The publication of more general reports or other documents could allow the ombudsmen to raise the profile of other aspects of their functions – such as improving governance in general.

7.16　The Parliamentary Commissioner "may from time to time lay before each House of Parliament such other reports with respect to [its] functions as he thinks fit".[6] Similar provision exists for the Health Service Ombudsman.[7]

---

[1]　Public Services Ombudsman (Wales) Act 2005, sch 1, para 14.

[2]　Standing Orders of the National Assembly for Wales, Ord 13.1(v).

[3]　Local Government Act 1974, s 23A(3A).

[4]　Local Government and Public Involvement in Health Act 2007, s 170(5). In force 1 April 2008 in relation to any report submitted on or after 1 April 2008.

[5]　Independent Housing Ombudsman Scheme, para 40.

7.17 The Public Services Ombudsman for Wales may prepare extraordinary reports, which can include general recommendations, and are laid before the National Assembly for Wales.[8]

7.18 There are no equivalent provisions for the Local Government Ombudsman or the Housing Ombudsman.

## RECENT DEVELOPMENTS

7.19 Here we consider the progress of what have become known as the Wright reforms, after Dr Tony Wright MP the then Chairman of the Public Administration Select Committee and Chairman of the House of Commons Reform Committee. We also consider recent academic work on pre-appointment hearings undertaken at the request of the Liaison Committee.

### The proposals made in the Wright report

7.20 With regard to select committees, the Wright Committee was tasked primarily with reforming the way in which chairs and members of select committees were chosen. However, the Committee also considered the time allocated to select committee reports in the House as part of its review of the control of House business in general.

7.21 The report noted with dissatisfaction that select committees had no special right of access to the House and were dependent on ministers and business managers to table their proposals and ensure that they were debated.[9] The Wright Committee therefore made a broad suggestion that select committees should be given greater access to the agenda so that their reports could be debated upon substantive motions in the House, at a time convenient to them. The report also made suggestions relating to more flexible use of time in Westminster Hall to allow for greater consideration of select committee reports.[10]

7.22 The report included these suggestions regarding the allocation of time in the context of its broader proposals on reform of the House's business. It, therefore, made no specific recommendations on this issue. However, the Wright Committee felt that the establishment of a Backbench Business Committee (and a House Business Committee) would allow for greater prioritisation of select committee work in the House.[11]

---

[6] Parliamentary Commissioner Act 1967, s 10(4).

[7] Health Service Commissioners Act 1993, s 14(4)(b).

[8] Public Services Ombudsman (Wales) Act 2005, sch 1, para 14(1)(b).

[9] Rebuilding the House, Report of the House of Commons Reform Committee (2008-09) HC 1117.

[10] Above, para 191.

[11] Above, paras 180 to 181.

### The proposals made by the Liaison Committee

7.23 In its report on the proposals made by the Wright Committee relating to select committees, the Liaison Committee endorsed – for the most part – the proposed changes.[12]

7.24 With regard to the time given over for debate and votes on select committee proposals, the Liaison Committee welcomed the idea of "House time" as an opportunity to allow backbenchers to call the Government to account over select committee reports.

7.25 However, the Liaison Committee expressed some caution with regards to greater presentation of select committee reports on the floor of the House. It felt that it would be unwise to use these opportunities to provoke ill-considered rebuttal from the Government rather than waiting for the formal response it was required to give within two months of a select committee report's publication.

### Implementation of the proposals

7.26 The Coalition Agreement stated the Government's intention to "bring forward the proposals of the Wright Committee", starting with the Backbench Business Committee.[13] This commitment was confirmed by the new Leader of the House, Sir George Young MP, in the first week of the new Parliament of 2010.[14]

### Establishment of the Backbench Business Committee

7.27 The debate on establishing a Backbench Business Committee for the House of Commons took place on 15 June 2010.[15] Introducing the debate, the Leader of the House stated the Government's aims:

> Today we are presenting the House with an opportunity to seize back some of the powers that have been taken away by the Government. We want to restore to back-bench Members greater control over the business of the House than they have had for not only a generation, but more than a century.[16]

7.28 At the conclusion of the debate, a Standing Order of the House of Commons was made establishing the Backbench Business Committee and ascribing powers to it.

7.29 The importance of this measure is that it gives Members of Parliament far greater control over Parliamentary time. The Backbench Business Committee will be able to determine what is debated in a portion of the total Parliamentary time – rather

---

[12] Rebuilding the House: Select Committee Issues, Report of the Liaison Committee (2009-10) HC 272.

[13] HM Government, *The Coalition: our programme for Government* (2010) p 27.

[14] *Hansard* (HC), 27 May 2010, vol 510, col 286.

[15] *Hansard* (HC), 15 June 2010, vol 511, cols 778 to 842.

[16] *Hansard* (HC), 15 June 2010, vol 511, col 778 (Leader of the House, Sir George Young MP).

than it all being controlled by the Whips, as has previously been the case.[17] This should allow the Backbench Business Committee to timetable a debate on a particular ombudsman report – should it so desire.

## CONCLUSIONS AND PROVISIONAL PROPOSALS

7.30 We suggest that current developments within Parliament could provide useful mechanisms for raising the profile of the work of the ombudsmen – either in general or in relation to an individual report.

7.31 It is not our place to make provisional proposals to reform the internal rules for elected bodies. What we can do is consider the legal ability for the public services ombudsmen to lay a report before Parliament or the National Assembly for Wales – thereby bringing it within that elected body's system.

7.32 In this project we have taken a broad approach to the public services ombudsmen – including the Housing Ombudsman. The current position concerning relationships with elected bodies does not reflect this approach. There is no defined role for Parliament in relation to the Housing Ombudsman.

7.33 Following recent changes to the Local Government Act 1974, in 2007, the current situation is that the Housing Ombudsman is now the only one of our public services ombudsmen that does not have to lay its annual report before an elected body. Given that the work of the Housing Ombudsman is likely to be of interest to Members in their constituency work – or in general – then we suggest that this is, at best, anomalous. **We provisionally propose that a duty is placed on the Housing Ombudsman to lay its annual reports before Parliament.**

7.34 Similarly, even where there is an existing relationship with an elected body, there is no consistency between those public services ombudsmen. The Local Government Ombudsman's relationship with Parliament is of a very different nature to that of the Parliamentary Commissioner and the Health Service Ombudsman.

7.35 We accept that there may be valid reasons for this, such as the fact that the Parliamentary Commissioner – in particular – can be seen as a tool of Parliament. However, in Part 6, we highlighted how publicity is at the core of the work of all of the public services ombudsmen. It is undeniable that having access to elected bodies is one of the ways of achieving this. Therefore, we think that the position of the Local Government Ombudsman and the Housing Ombudsman should be strengthened, so as to give them similar access to this valuable resource as enjoyed by the other public services ombudsmen.

7.36 **We provisionally propose that the governing statutes for the Local Government Ombudsman and the Housing Ombudsman be amended to allow them to lay the full range of their reports resulting from investigations before Parliament, in a similar manner to the Parliamentary Commissioner or the Health Service Ombudsman.**

---

[17] *Hansard* (HC), 15 June 2010, vol 511, col 782 (Leader of the House, Sir George Young MP).

7.37    The creation of a power to lay reports before Parliament could potentially impose extra costs and administrative burdens on both the body laying the report and Parliament. Therefore, it is necessary to justify the creation of a power in all cases. We are of the opinion that this would be worthwhile in the case of individual reports, given our conclusion as to the importance of publicity in securing implementation. However, we are not convinced there needs to be a change in relation to general reports or other documents issued by the Local Government Ombudsman or the Housing Ombudsman. Consequently, we are not going to make any provisional proposals in relation to these.

7.38    In relation to the Public Services Ombudsman for Wales, we suggest that the current relationship with the National Assembly for Wales is entirely appropriate.

# PART 8
# SUMMARY OF SPECIFIC POINTS FOR CONSULTATION

## INTRODUCTION

8.1 This Part collates the specific points for consultation set out in the main body of this consultation paper in one place.

## PART 3: APPOINTMENT OF OMBUDSMEN

8.2 We provisionally propose that Parliament nominate to the Queen a candidate for the post of Parliamentary Commissioner for Administration. (paragraph 3.34)

## PART 4: OPENING AN OMBUDSMAN INVESTIGATION

### Statutory bar

8.3 We provisionally propose that the existing statutory bars be reformed. We provisionally propose that there is a general presumption in favour of a public services ombudsman being able to open a complaint. (paragraph 4.42)

8.4 Do consultees agree that there should be a general presumption in favour of the ombudsman being able to investigate a complaint coupled with a broad discretion to decline to open an investigation? (paragraph 4.47)

8.5 Do consultees agree that in deciding whether to exercise their discretion to decline to open an investigation ombudsmen should ask themselves whether the complainant has already had or should have had recourse to a court or tribunal? (paragraph 4.47)

### Stay of proceedings

8.6 We provisionally propose that there should be a stay and transfer power allowing matters to be transferred from the courts to the public services ombudsmen. (paragraph 4.76)

8.7 Do consultees agree that the court should invite submissions from the original parties before transferring the matter? (paragraph 4.77)

8.8 Do consultees agree that, in the event of such a transfer, the ombudsman should be obliged to open an investigation? (paragraph 4.78)

8.9 Do consultees agree that the ombudsman should also be able to abandon the investigation should it – in their opinion – not disclose maladministration? (paragraph 4.79)

### Alternatives to investigation

8.10 We provisionally propose that the Parliamentary Commissioner, the Local Government Ombudsman and the Health Service Ombudsman be given specific powers to allow them to dispose of complaints in ways other than by conducting an investigation. (paragraph 4.85)

### Formal requirements

8.11 We provisionally propose that a discretionary provision relating to formal requirements, similar to section 26B(3) of the Local Government Act 1974, be inserted into the governing statutes for the Parliamentary Commissioner and the Health Service Ombudsman, excluding the Housing Ombudsman. This would allow them to dispense with the requirement that a complaint be in writing. (paragraph 4.91)

### MP filter

8.12 We provisionally propose that a dual-track approach to reform of the MP filter be adopted by Parliament. (paragraph 4.106)

## PART 5: OMBUDSMEN INVESTIGATIONS

### Closed nature of ombudsmen investigations

8.13 We provisionally propose that there should be statutory discretion for the public services ombudsmen to dispense with the requirement that an investigation be conducted in private in situations where they see this as appropriate. (paragraph 5.33)

8.14 Do consultees think that, if such discretion were created, the public services ombudsmen should be protected from additional burdens? (paragraph 5.34)

8.15 If so, would consultees prefer a more general exemption from the duty contained in section 1 of Freedom of Information Act 2000 in relation to investigations, as is currently the case? Alternatively, would consultees prefer a more limited exemption modelled on section 36(5)(ka) of the Freedom of Information Act 2000? (paragraph 5.35)

### Reference on a point of law

8.16 Before making a reference to a court on a point of law, should there be a requirement that the public services ombudsmen seek either the opinion of or arbitration by an independent counsel? (paragraph 5.83)

8.17 We provisionally propose that the counsel's fees should be met by the public services ombudsmen. (paragraph 5.84)

8.18 We provisionally propose that the there should be a mechanism allowing a public services ombudsman to ask a question of the Administrative Court. (paragraph 5.85)

8.19 We provisionally propose that such a reference should not require permission. (paragraph 5.86)

8.20 We provisionally propose that the decision of the Administrative Court on such a matter should be considered a judgment of the Court for the purposes of section 16 of the Senior Courts Act 1981 and, therefore, potentially subject to appeal to the Court of Appeal. (paragraph 5.87)

8.21    We provisionally propose that the public services ombudsmen should notify the complainant and the relevant public bodies of their intention to make a referral on a point of law, invite them to submit their views and/or to intervene before the court should they wish to. (paragraph 5.88)

8.22    We provisionally propose that the final decision whether to refer a question to the court should be solely that for the public services ombudsman. (paragraph 5.89)

8.23    Should the ombudsman routinely instruct one counsel to put both sides of the question or should two opposing counsel be instructed? (paragraph 5.90)

8.24    We provisionally propose that other interested parties may intervene, subject to case management decisions of the court. (paragraph 5.91)

8.25    We provisionally propose that, subject to the use of costs orders for case management purposes, the default position should be all parties or interveners – including the public services ombudsmen – should meet their own costs. (paragraph 5.92)

## PART 6: REPORTING

### Types of report

8.26    Do consultees agree that adopting a graduated approach to three different types of report, based on that already in place for the Public Services Ombudsman for Wales, would be desirable for each of the public services ombudsmen except the Housing Ombudsman? (paragraph 6.82)

8.27    Do consultees agree that these should be known as "short-form report", "report" and "special report"? (paragraph 6.83)

8.28    We provisionally propose that in order to ensure greater transparency, where the public ombudsmen decline to commence an investigation, or decide to abandon an existing investigation, there should be a statutory requirement to publish a "statement of reasons", setting out clearly the reasons for their decision. (paragraph 6.84)

8.29    We provisionally propose that the Housing Ombudsman's determinations should be recast as reports where they relate to social housing. (paragraph 6.85)

8.30    We provisionally propose that ombudsmen should routinely ask complainants whether they want to be anonymous. (paragraph 6.86)

8.31    We provisionally propose that the ombudsmen should not be able to identify a complainant or other individual without their consent. (paragraph 6.86)

### Findings and recommendations

8.32    Do consultees agree that the governing statutes should draw a distinction between findings and recommendations and use those terms? (paragraph 6.89)

8.33    We provisionally propose that there should be a statutory definition for findings. This should include findings of fact and whether there was maladministration and injustice. (paragraph 6.90)

### Status of findings and recommendations

8.34    We provisionally conclude that the proper approach to recommendations is as part of the political process. (paragraph 6.95)

8.35    We provisionally propose that a public body should only be able to reject the findings in a report of a public services ombudsman following the successful judicial review of that report. (paragraph 6.107)

### Issuing general reports

8.36    Do consultees agree that there should be a specific statutory power for each of the public services ombudsmen to publish guidance, principles of good administration and codes of practice? (paragraph 6.115)

### PART 7: RELATIONSHIP WITH ELECTED BODIES

8.37    We provisionally propose that a duty is placed on the Housing Ombudsman to lay its annual reports before Parliament. (paragraph 7.33)

8.38    We provisionally propose that the governing statutes for the Local Government Ombudsman and the Housing Ombudsman be amended to allow them to lay the full range of their reports resulting from investigations before Parliament, in a similar manner to the Parliamentary Commissioner or the Health Service Ombudsman. (paragraph 7.36)

# APPENDIX A
# IMPACT ASSESSMENT

A.1 This Appendix sets out the reasoning that informs our impact assessment for this consultation paper. The full impact assessment itself is available from our website.

A.2 Here we discuss the costs and benefits of our proposals in both monetised and non-monetised terms. At this stage in the project, we are seeking to assess the general parameters for our provisionally proposed reforms. When we publish our subsequent report, we will set out a more detailed cost benefit analysis. We ask consultees to comment on the impact of our provisional proposals to assist with this process.

A.3 We have adjusted the figures in this cost benefit analysis to 2009-10 figures using the Gross Domestic Product (GDP) deflator.[1] This is in accordance with HM Treasury guidance. The figure taken for the change between the reporting year 2008-09 and that of 2009-10 is 1.51%.[2] Figures have been rounded to pounds.

A.4 Net present values in this impact assessment are calculated over 10 years in 2009-10 prices, and discounted at the approved rate of 3.5%. We have assumed that the costs and benefits start to accrue in year 1, and stop in year 10.

## COSTS AND BENEFITS

A.5 Impact assessments identify both monetised and non-monetised impacts on individuals, groups, businesses and the public sector, with the aim of giving a picture of what the overall impact to society might be from implementing the provisional proposals.

A.6 Impact assessments place a strong emphasis on valuing the costs and benefits in monetary terms. We considers the costs and benefits for Option 1 against the base case of Option 0 – which is leaving the current regime as is, the "do nothing option". We do this principally in terms of on-going costs and benefits.

A.7 The purpose of our provisional proposals is to reform and improve the system of the public services ombudsmen. In certain instances this means transferring matters currently dealt with by courts or tribunals to the public services ombudsmen. We have not provisionally proposed reform to the substantive law relating to the matters that ombudsmen consider, for instance the definition of maladministration.

A.8 There will, of course, be transitional costs. However, given the open nature of many of our consultation questions, we are not able to quantify these at present. We would not, in any event, expect any transitional costs to be significant. To the extent that there are transitional costs, these would result primarily from minor

---

[1] The GDP deflator is a measure of the level of prices of all new, domestically produced, final goods and services in an economy. It is equal to nominal GDP divided by real GDP, multiplied by 100.

[2] See http://www.hm-treasury.gov.uk/data_gdp_fig.htm (last visited 16 August 2010).

changes to administrative practice and consequent training.

A.9　There are, however, other important aspects of our provisional proposals that cannot be monetised sensibly. These include how the provisional proposals impact differently on particular groups in society or improve equity and fairness. Where non-monetised costs or benefits need to be considered, we have highlighted them.

**General costs**

A.10　Throughout this impact assessment, we need to use two sets of figures. These are, first, the costs of disposing of a complaint by the public services ombudsmen. Second is the cost of the equivalent action to an ombudsman complaint before a court.

*Cost of disposing of a complaint*

A.11　Based on the reporting year 2008-09 we consider the cost of disposing of complaints by each of the public services ombudsmen.[3] We deal with the ombudsmen separately as they report in different ways. Figures are adjusted by the GDP deflator to 2009-10 prices.

LOCAL GOVERNMENT OMBUDSMAN

A.12　The figure supplied by the Local Government Ombudsman for the cost of disposing of an individual complaint in 2009-10 is £689. This figure is calculated as the average cost of both the complaints dealt with by an investigative team and prematurely made complaints.

PARLIAMENTARY COMMISSIONER AND HEALTH SERVICE OMBUDSMAN

A.13　We consider these ombudsmen together as their annual accounts are published jointly. The Parliamentary Commissioner and the Health Service Ombudsman do not record the average cost of disposing of complaints. However, we think it is reasonable to derive a figure by analogy with the Local Government Ombudsman. The Local Government Ombudsman sends to its investigative teams 11,687 complaints, and removes 5,974 as premature. Therefore, the total budget for complaints comes to is £12,168,429 ((11,687 + 5,974) x £689). The overall budget for the Local Government Ombudsman is £14,276,366.

A.14　The proportion of their budget going on the handing of complaints by investigative teams is 0.852347789 (£12,168,429 / £14,276,366). The assumption that we make is that this relationship between the total budget and the budget for disposing of individual complaints is the same for the other public services ombudsmen. We think that this is a defensible assumption, given the broad similarities in their activities.

A.15　The overall budget for the Parliamentary Commissioner and Health Service Ombudsman in the reporting year 2008-09 was £26,489,075 (in 2009-10 prices). Applying the ratio for the relationship between the total budget and the budget for

---

[3]　Figures taken from: Local Government Ombudsman, *Annual Report 2008-09, Delivering public value* (2008-09); Every complaint matters, Annual Report of the Parliamentary and Health Service Ombudsman (2008-09) HC 786.

disposing of individual complaints taken from the Local Government Ombudsman, this means that the individual disposals budget was £22,577,905.

A.16    In that same year, some 8,737 complaints were considered.[4] This we take as the total number of complaints less those dismissed as "not properly made", for instance where a complaint to the Parliamentary Commissioner had not come from a Member of Parliament or was not made in writing. Therefore, for the purposes of this impact assessment, we will take the average cost of disposing of an individual complaint by the Parliamentary Commissioner or Health Service Ombudsman as £2,584 (£22,577,905 / 8,737), adjusted for 2010.

PUBLIC SERVICES OMBUDSMAN FOR WALES

A.17    It is possible to generate similar figures for the Public Services Ombudsman for Wales. The 2008-09 overall budget was £3,148,840 (in 2009-10 prices). Applying the ratio between overall budget and the budget for complaint disposal from the Local Government Ombudsman, this makes the budget for individual complaints £2,683,907. The number of substantive complaints disposed of was 1,422.[5] This makes the cost of individual disposals £1,887 (£2,683,907 / 1,422).

HOUSING OMBUDSMAN

A.18    The final figure that we can derive is the average cost of disposing of a complaint by the Housing Ombudsman. There are particular issues here, as the Housing Ombudsman's accounts do not disaggregate between the cost of investigations into social housing complaints and those relating to the private sector. For the purposes of this impact assessment we assume that the costs are broadly similar, as their private sector work accounts for a very small percentage of their overall work.

A.19    The 2008-09 budget was £3,004,081 (in 2009-10 prices). Applying the Local Government Ombudsman ratio, this gives an investigative budget of £2,560,522. In 2008-09 3,870 complaints were disposed of. This gives a cost per disposal of £662 (2,560,522 / 3,870).

A.20    Therefore, in tabular form, this is as follows.

| Public services ombudsman | Average cost of considering complaint |
|---|---|
| Local Government Ombudsman | £689 |
| Parliamentary Commissioner | £2,584 |
| Health Service Ombudsman | |
| Public Services Ombudsman for Wales | £1,887 |
| Housing Ombudsman | £662 |

[4]    Every complaint matters, Annual Report of the Parliamentary and Health Service Ombudsman (2008-09) HC 786, p 9.
[5]    Public Services Ombudsman for Wales, *Annual Report 2008-09* (2009) p 15.

### Court costs

A.21 We take the figures from the impact assessment accompanying our report on High Court Jurisdiction.[6] There we gave the administrative costs and the costs of instructing counsel for a half-day hearing in the Administrative Court as £8,000. These figures were in 2008-09 prices, representing £8,121 in 2009-10 prices. For the purposes of this impact assessment we will take a full-day hearing as £16,242, including junior counsel.

A.22 In the High Court Jurisdiction impact assessment, we took the costs of an application for permission to bring judicial review proceedings including judicial time and other overheads as £126 and the administrative costs of a half-day substantive hearing as £487. This means that the total administrative costs of a half-day hearing including the granting of permission comes to £613 in 2008-09 prices, or £622 in 2009-10 prices. Therefore, for this project, we take the administrative costs of a full day hearing as £1,117 ((£126 + (2 x £487)) x 1.0151).

A.23 There is also a point where the costs of a county court action, especially in housing matters, should be considered. We have taken such actions as a half day (3.5 hour) hearing, with a half day preparation time. Taking commercial rates for junior counsel as £150/hour,[7] the cost, assuming equal representation on both sides is £2,100 (2 x 150 x (3.5 + 3.5)). A full day would, therefore, cost £4,200.

A.24 To work out the court costs, we have taken the cost of the county court (£209,157,517) and divided it by the number of days sat (149,467).[8] This makes the cost of the country court per day sat £1,399. We have taken our half day figure as £700.

A.25 The combination of the two gives an overall cost for a half day in the county court of £2,800 (£2,100 + £700). Similarly a full day in the county court is estimated to cost £5,599 (£4,200 + £1,399).

| Court | Average cost of half day (junior counsel) | Average cost of day (junior counsel) |
|---|---|---|
| Administrative Court | £8,121 | £16,242 |
| County court | £2,800 | £5,599 |

[6] The High Court's jurisdiction in relation to criminal proceedings (2010) Law Com No 324, Appendix D.

[7] Figures supplied by the Legal Services Commission. Here we are assuming the use of counsel under 5 years call.

[8] Figures supplied by Her Majesty's Courts Service. Costs include maintenance costs, variable costs, semi-variable costs and staff costs.

**Reform of the statutory bar**

A.26 The Local Government Ombudsman rejected 352 complaints in 2008-09 on the basis of the statutory bar.[9]

A.27 The Parliamentary Commissioner and the Health Service Ombudsman jointly rejected 39 complaints during the reporting year 2008-09 due to the operation of the statutory bar.[10]

A.28 For the Public Services Ombudsman for Wales, 8 complaints were disposed of in this manner during 2008-09.

A.29 Having contacted the office of the Housing Ombudsman, we do not think that it loses complaints due to the operation of its equivalent to the statutory bar.

*Costs*

A.30 The maximum possible cost is where all the cases currently rejected due to the application of the statutory bar go to the appropriate public services ombudsman.

A.31 This does not necessarily mean that they will become full investigations, as many will still be rejected for other reasons, such as through application of the ombudsmen's general discretion. One key assumption that we make is that these complaints are currently rejected through the operation of the statutory bar at an early stage of the ombudsman process. Therefore the majority of the average costs of handling a complaint would normally accrue subsequent to any decision on whether to reject a complaint on the basis of the statutory bar. On this basis, we are going to take the additional cost of a complaint not being rejected on the basis of the statutory bar as the average cost of a complaint.

A.32 The maximum annual cost for the Local Government Ombudsman is £242,528 (352 x £689). The maximum cost for the Parliamentary Commissioner and Health Service Ombudsman is £100,783 (39 x £2,584). The maximum cost for the Public Services Ombudsman for Wales is £15,099 (8 x £1,887). Therefore, the total maximum cost for these public services ombudsmen is £358,410.

A.33 The minimum annual cost would be £0. This would be where reform does not lead to any change in current practice, in that the complaints are still rejected at a preliminary stage, rather than being disposed of later on in the process.

A.34 There is also the possibility that reform of the statutory bars would generate new complaints. Currently complainants may be advised not to use the public services ombudsmen but rather to go to court, as a result of the statutory bars. These complainants would not be included in the statistics of rejected complaints, but if the statutory bars were reformed then such complainants may chose to have recourse to the ombudsmen. This would, therefore, create additional burdens for the ombudsmen. However, we do not think that the reform would lead to any significant number of new claims. Consequently, we have not included these in out calculations.

[9] Figures supplied by the Local Government Ombudsman.
[10] Figures supplied by the Parliamentary Commissioner and the Health Service Ombudsman.

A.35    The best estimate is that, rather than being rejected at a preliminary stage, complaints are all treated alike. Therefore, we suggest that the best estimate of the annual cost should be taken as the full figure of £358,410.

**Benefits**

A.36    The maximum possible benefit is the consequent reduction of judicial review or other court actions. It is, of course, not a given that cases rejected by the ombudsmen on the basis of the statutory bars will go to court. Furthermore, where complaints are rejected we think that some cases may go to the county court rather than the Administrative Court – especially in the case of the Local Government Ombudsman where the complaint relates to housing.

A.37    To give the range we have used the Administrative Court costs for a full day hearing. Therefore, the maximum benefit for reform of the Local Government Ombudsman statutory bar is £5,717,043 (352 x £16,242). The maximum benefit for reform of the Parliamentary Commissioner and the Health Service Ombudsman statutory bar is £633,422 (39 x £16,242). The maximum benefit for reform of the Public Services Ombudsman for Wales statutory bar is £129,933 (8 x £16,242). Therefore, the total maximum benefit in respect of these ombudsmen is £6,480,398.

A.38    The minimum possible benefit is £0. This would be where there is no change to the current situation and the reform has no actual effect on current practice.

A.39    We suggest that the best estimate would be much lower than the maximum possible benefit figures. There are several reasons for this. First, as stated above, claims rejected on the basis of the statutory bar do not necessarily go to courts. Where rejected complaints do not proceed to court, any reform would not lead to cases being taken back from the courts. We estimate that only 25% of claims rejected on the basis of the statutory bar would be suitable for a court. This gives a much smaller figure for benefits. Second, we suggest that it is appropriate to adjust the estimate on the basis that half of the cases relating to the public services ombudsmen will be taken from the county court rather than the Administrative Court. Third, we estimate that half will be full day and half only require a half day in court. These are, of course, assumptions that we will discuss over the course of consultation.

A.40    For the Local Government Ombudsman the best estimate of the annual benefit is £720,752.[11] The figure for the Parliamentary and Health Service Ombudsmen is £79,856.[12] The best estimate for the Public Services Ombudsman for Wales is £16,381.[13] Therefore, our best estimate of the annual benefits is £816,988.

A.41    Additional non-monetised benefits are that an ombudsman's investigation is likely to be swifter, that it would not necessitate the potential emotional distress that going to court can cause some people and that there is a greater possibility of a monetary remedy being awarded to the individual complainant.

---

[11]   (22 x £2,800) + (22 x £5,599) + (22 x £16,242) + (22 x £8,121).

[12]   (2.5 x £2,800) + (2.5 x £5,599) + (2.5 x £16,242) + (2.5 x £8,121).

[13]   (0.5 x £2,800) + (0.5 x £5,599) + (0.5 x £16,242) + (0.5 x £8,121).

### Net impact

A.42    In tabular form, this is as follows.

|  | High | Low | Best estimate |
|---|---|---|---|
| Annual Cost | £358,410 | £0 | £358,410 |
| Annual Benefit | £6,480,398 | £0 | £816,988 |
| **Net benefit** | | | **£458,578** |
| **Net present value** | | | **£3,813,814** |

### Dedicated powers to stay court proceedings and transfer matters to an ombudsman

A.43    We estimate that there would be some 10 to 50 judicial review cases per year where this stay and transfer power would operate. Any benefit to this would be the saving from moving a case out of the Administrative Court to an ombudsman less the additional costs imposed on the ombudsman by having to investigate the case.

### Costs

A.44    The maximum costs of this would be where 50 new investigations are considered by the most expensive of the public services ombudsmen, the Parliamentary Commissioner and the Health Service Ombudsman. This, therefore, comes to £129,209 (50 x £2,584).

A.45    It is theoretically possible that the minimum costs are £0, where no complaints are actually investigated by the ombudsmen to whom the matters are transferred. However, we take as our minimum costs that 10 matters are investigated by the cheapest of the public services ombudsmen, the Local Government Ombudsman. This gives a figure of £6,890 (£689 x 10).

A.46    Our best estimate is to take the middle figure, 30, and allocate this in the same way that current complaints are distributed as between the ombudsmen. As with the earlier figure, we do not think that this will affect the Housing Ombudsmen, as their primary jurisdiction does not cover the sort of matters that tend to come before the Administrative Court.

A.47    Taking the figures for 2008-09, there were 27,820 complaints disposed of by the public services ombudsmen considered here, of which 17,661 went to the Local Government Ombudsman, 8,737 to the Parliamentary Commissioner and Health Service Ombudsman and 1,422 to the Public Services Ombudsman for Wales. Applying these proportions to the 30 cases to be stayed and transferred, this would mean 19 cases going to the Local Government Ombudsman, 9 to the Parliamentary Commissioner and Health Service Ombudsman and 2 to the Public Services Ombudsman for Wales.

A.48 To calculate the cost these numbers should be multiplied by the cost of disposing of a complaint before the relevant ombudsman. Therefore the best estimate costs are £40,373 ((19 x £689) + (9 x £2,584) + (2 x £1,887)).

### *Benefits*

A.49 The maximum benefit would be where 50 cases are transferred from the Administrative Court and the minimum benefit is where 10 are transferred from the same court. This gives a range from £81,208 (10 x £8,121) to £406,040 (50 x £8,121).

A.50 Taking the best estimate as 30 cases again, and assuming that these are from half day hearings, then the best estimate of the possible benefit to reform is £243,624.

A.51 There is a potential reduction to this where cases return to the Administrative Court after being investigated by the public services ombudsman as there are still issue that need to be dealt with by the Court. However, we do not see this is particularly likely.

A.52 There are other non-monetised benefits that should be considered here, which would be the same as those for the reform of the statutory bar.

### *Net impact*

|  | High | Low | Best estimate |
|---|---|---|---|
| Annual Cost | £129,209 | £6,890 | £40,373 |
| Annual Benefit | £406,040 | £81,208 | £243,624 |
| **Net benefit** |  |  | **£203,251** |
| **Net present value** |  |  | **£1,690,356** |

### Specific powers for the ombudsmen to use alternative means for dispute resolution

A.53 Given the way in which the ombudsmen report, and that the use of mediators is a relatively recent development, we feel unable to monetise this. Whilst we can see advantages in having a specific statutory power to do this, it is true that – in relation to mediation – then the ombudsmen can already do this.

A.54 The costs would be the additional costs of using a mediator or other form of alternative dispute resolution. The benefits would be the money saved by not proceeding with an investigation.

### Amendment to the formal requirements for making a complaint

A.55 Unfortunately, whilst we can see advantages to this, it is hard to monetise them. In preliminary discussions on this issue with the Local Government Ombudsman, they have said that they greatly appreciate the recent changes to their regime, such that the formal requirement for a written complaint can be dispensed with.

The effect of this change has been to alter the way in which they receive complaints. Taking the figures supplied for 2009-10, telephone complaints now form the majority of complaints received (40,200), with e-mail next (30,440) and written postal complaints a distant third (12,836). This, we suggest, reflects general trends in society and is something that should be embraced by the legislative schemes for the Parliamentary Commissioner and the Health Service Ombudsman.

A.56    In our final impact assessment, if we proceed with this provisional proposal, we hope to give more specific costs and benefits. This is an issue on which we aim to consult.

**Reform of the MP filter**

A.57    In the reporting year 2007-08, 756 complaints were referred back to the complainant for MP referral. Of these, 400 were closed as the complainant failed to obtain referral from an MP. In 2008-09, 580 complaints were referred back, with 225 of these being closed due to the complainant failing to obtain referral from an MP.[14]

A.58    Therefore, there were 225 "lost" complaints in 2008-09. The greatest possible burden would be that all of those complaints proceeded to be considered by the Parliamentary Commissioner.

*Costs*

A.59    The minimum, maximum and best estimate of the cost, we think, are the costs of disposing of the "lost" 225 complaints as if they were other complaints. This comes to £581,439 (225 x £2,584).

A.60    While complaints increased when the councillor filter for the Local Government Ombudsman was removed, we do not think that it is appropriate as a model for the impact of reform in relation to the MP filter. In that case there were specific problems which do not apply here as the Parliamentary Commissioner has already taken extensive steps to reduce the adverse impact of the MP filter.

*Benefits*

A.61    We do not think it practicable to monetise the benefits. There would be a reduction in delay for complainants and public bodies and a potential reduction in the administrative costs of Members of Parliament.

*Net impact*

|  | **High** | **Low** | **Best estimate** |
|---|---|---|---|
| Annual Cost | £581,439 | £581,439 | £581,439 |
| **Net present value** |  |  | **-£4,835,595** |

[14] Figures supplied by the Parliamentary Commissioner.

**Power to make a reference to a court on a point of law**

A.62    We think that there would be no more than 2 to 3 of these a year. Of course, it may be that in some years there are no references made, either because a problematic issue does not arise or because the matter is dealt with by other means, for instance on the basis of an opinion sought from counsel. In this consultation paper we have left open whether there should be two sets of opposing counsel instructed or whether a single set of counsel should put both sides of a question to the court.

A.63    Having discussed the matter with the Legal Services Commission, we think that the time allocation for a reference would reasonably be 2 days research, 1 day case preparation and 1 day in court. We have taken the rate for senior counsel as £300 per hour and £150 per hour for a junior.[15] Therefore, one set of counsel would cost £13,500 ((300 x 4 x 7.5) + (150 x 4 x 7.5)).

A.64    We have also taken the figures from the High Court Jurisdiction Impact Assessment, this gives Court fees as £1,117 (in 2009-10 prices) for a full-day.

*Costs of a single set of counsel*

A.65    To calculate the potential range then the minimum figure would be £0, where no references are made. The maximum would be 3 full-day hearings, therefore, £43,851 (3 x (£1,117 + £13,500)).

*Costs of two sets of counsel*

A.66    The minimum is £0, again where no references are made. The maximum is three full day hearing and two sets of counsel, therefore £84,351 (3 x (£1,117 + (2 x £13,500))).

*Best estimate for reforms and total range for potential reform*

A.67    Our best estimate is that there would be two of these references a year. Given the open nature of our consultation question then with two sets of counsel this would be £56,234 (2 x (£1,117 + (2 x £13,500))). With a single set of counsel, this comes to £29,234 (2 x (£1,117 + £13,500)). For the purposes of this impact assessment, we have taken the best estimate to be the median figure of £42,734.

*Benefits*

A.68    The key benefits that we can see would be the improvement in the quality of ombudsmen's reports on specific legal issues and preventing them from having to discontinue an investigation where a difficult legal issue arises. However, we do not think it is possible to monetise these benefits.

---

[15] Here we take this as a junior of under 5 years call.

*Net impact*

|  | High | Low | Best estimate |
|---|---|---|---|
| Annual Cost | £84,351 | £0 | £42,734 |
| Net present value |  |  | -£355,402 |

### Modernising the system for issuing reports on individual investigations

A.69 We do not think that this particular change would have any significant cost implications. This is a change to the system for reporting and a requirement to release information already generated.

A.70 There are however non-monetised benefits to the provisional proposal, such as increased accessibility, accountability and transparency.

### Reform of the status of findings and recommendations

A.71 This is a legislative change to the current legal position, as held by the Court of Appeal. The purpose of doing this is to ensure that an ombudsman's findings are protected from mere dismissal by those subject to a report by the public services ombudsmen. We do not think it would have overall costs implications as we are not altering the status of recommendations.

A.72 There is a potential benefit, in that undertaking this reform could remove the need for future litigation. We do not feel able to predict the likelihood of that happening nor to monetise this.

### Specific power to issue general reports

A.73 Here we are suggesting a specific power to do what, in some cases, is already done. We see this as a codification of current practice. We do not, therefore, see it as having costs implications.

### Changes to the closed nature of ombudsmen hearings

A.74 We can see that there are possible costs implications in relation to this discretion. However, we do not feel able to quantify these. Our provisional proposal creates a power to do something but we do not, at this stage in the process, feel able to predict how that would in fact be used. Therefore, we treat this as an options proposal and will seek to ascertain potential costs in the context of our consultation.

A.75 There are non-monetised benefits to the provisional proposal, such as increased accessibility, accountability and transparency.

**Appointment of the Parliamentary Commissioner by Parliament**

A.76 We do not see this as creating significant additional costs. There is already a recruitment process for the Parliamentary Commissioner and Parliament has already stated that it will conduct pre-appointment hearings for the next Parliamentary Commissioner.

A.77 We do not think that any change would lead to additional costs to the public. Though there would be additional burdens in terms of select committee time – and time for the House sitting to approve a nomination – we think that these would be internalised within the normal budget for the work of Parliament. They would not, therefore, increase the burden placed on the public.

A.78 We will, however, explore this matter in greater detail during our consultation.

## PROVISIONAL CONCLUSIONS

A.79 In this consultation impact assessment we are seeking to set the broad parameters of our provisional proposals. We intend to develop more detailed figures over the course of our consultation.

A.80 There are also certain changes where we do not think that it is possible – or correct – to give figures, as any change would be internalised to an institution. Such theoretical costs or benefits cannot really be seen as such, in that there would be no actual change to the budget of the institution concerned. This may well be the case with the reform of the MP filter and certain issues – such as select committee sittings – in the case of appointment by Parliament of the Parliamentary Commissioner.

A.81 The table below collate the ranges calculated above, namely the costs and benefits of the reform of the statutory bar, dedicated powers to stay court proceedings and transfer matters to an ombudsman, reform of the MP filter, and power to make a reference to a court on a point of law. The table gives annual figures at 2009-10 prices.

**Annual monetised figures at 2009-10 prices**

|  | High | Low | Best estimate |
|---|---|---|---|
| Annual Cost | £1,153,409 | £588,329 | £1,022,956 |
| Annual Benefit | £6,886,438 | £81,208 | £1,060,612 |
| **Net benefit** |  |  | **£37,656** |
| **Net present value** |  |  | **£313,173** |

A.82 These figures do not take into account all of the non-monetised benefits of our provisional proposals. These include: greater access to the ombudsmen, strengthening mechanisms for administrative justice, and allowing for the closure of on-going complaints.